THE REAPPEARANCE OF CHRIST IN THE ETHERIC

The Reappearance of Christ in the Etheric

Selected Lectures by

RUDOLF STEINER

STEINERBOOKS

See page 237 for notes on this collection of lectures.

© Copyright SteinerBooks, 2003
Introduction © copyright Stephen E. Usher, 2003

Published in the United States by
SteinerBooks
PO Box 799, MA 01230

Library of Congress Cataloging-in-Publication Data

Steiner, Rudolf, 1861–1925.
   [Selections. English. 2003]
   The reappearance of Christ in the etheric : selected lectures by /
Rudolf Steiner ; introduced by Stephen E. Usher.
        p. cm.
   Includes bibliographical references.
   ISBN 0-88010-519-4 (alk. paper)
   1. Jesus Christ—Anthroposophical interpretations. I. Usher, Stephen,
1931- II. Title.
BP596.J4S75213 2003
299'.935—dc21
                                                    2003005524

10 9 8 7 6 5 4 3 2 1

Printed in the United States of America

· Contents

Introduction by Stephen E. Usher   *vi*

Publisher's Note   *xvii*

1. The Appearance of Christ in the Etheric   *1*

2. Spiritual Science and Etheric Vision   *26*

3. Buddhism and Pauline Christianity   *47*

4. Mysteries of the Universe: Comets and the Moon   *54*

5. The Reappearance of Christ in the Etheric   *72*

6. The Sermon on the Mount and the Land of Shambhala   *92*

7. The Return of Christ   *106*

8. The Etheric Vision of the Future   *114*

9. The Etherization of the Blood   *122*

10. Spirit Beings and the Ground of the World – 1   *146*

11. Spirit Beings and the Ground of the World – 2   *170*

12. Spirit Beings and the Ground of the World – 3   *189*

13. The Three Realms between Death and Rebirth   *209*

Further Reading   *234*

· Introduction

Stephen E. Usher

This volume contains a series of lectures delivered by Rudolf
Steiner to different audiences in Europe during 1910, 1911,
and 1917. These audiences were familiar with and sympathetic
to Rudolf Steiner's world conception. In particular, they understood what a person could learn from a study of Steiner's *Outline of Esoteric Science.*[1] In that volume Rudolf Steiner
introduces the idea that a science of the spirit, in contrast to
natural science, is a cultural activity that is not only possible
but also vitally important to the future of mankind. Regarding
the discoveries of spiritual science, the third statute of the
Anthroposophical Society[2] states that,

> No special degree of academic learning is required to make
> them one's own and to found one's life upon them, but only
> an open-minded human nature. Research into these results,
> however, as well as competent evaluation of them, depends
> upon spiritual-scientific training, which is to be acquired
> step by step. These results are in their own way as exact as the

---

1. Anthroposophic Press, 1997.
2. Rudolf Steiner formulated the statutes at the Christmas Foundation meeting
of the Anthroposophical Society that took place during December 1923 and January 1924.

results of genuine natural science. When they attain general recognition in the same way as these, they will bring about comparable progress in all spheres of life, not only in the spiritual but also in the practical realm.[3]

The training of a spiritual scientist proceeds along exactly specified lines and brings about the further development of his soul-spiritual being, a process that might require several incarnations. This development can be compared to the development of a human being from fertilized egg to adult, but here the development takes place in the soul and spirit of the aspiring spiritual researcher and the development is undertaken consciously.[4] The result of this development is the capacity for precise clairvoyant observation and understanding of the spiritual world. The training makes the student into an instrument for observing the spiritual world and thereby capable of spiritual-scientific research.

When a modern spiritual researcher wishes to convey his discoveries he first translates them into conceptual form. The resulting communications are comprehensible to anyone capable of unprejudiced thinking. In reality this is not possible for many people because they are so immersed in the dominant materialistic worldview of our time.

In the following analogy, Steiner describes the difficulties that arise when people with a materialistic worldview approach the findings of spiritual science. Suppose a person could not read and decided to study a book. He could make all kinds of

---

3. Rudolf Steiner, *The Christmas Conference for the Foundation of the General Anthroposophical Society 1923/1924* (Anthroposophic Press, 1990), p. 58.
4. See, for example, Rudolf Steiner, *How to Know Higher Worlds: The Classic Guide to the Spiritual Journey* (Anthroposophic Press, 2002; GA 10).

observations about the shape and ordering of the letters on the page, but he would find incredible that something else, say Shakespeare's *King Lear*, could be found there. If he debated about the page with a person who knew how to read he might well make fun, stating that nothing of the kind was to be found there but rather only black letters on a white background.

A related problem is applying a materialistic scientific approach in a domain where it is inadequate to the task. A particularly striking example of this problem is found in the area of New Testament scholarship. Through spiritual scientific research Steiner discovered that it is in the very nature of the Mystery of Golgotha that no outer historical research will ever be able to prove that it happened, much less what it was really about. This is possible only for spiritual science. Steiner puts it this way in the last lecture of this volume:

> Those who refuse to grasp the Mystery of Golgotha through a spiritual understanding of earthly evolution—without historical documents—will never understand it at all. This is the will of the gods, so to speak. Regarding the most important event on earth, human beings must exert spiritual activity. The Mystery of Golgotha can always be refuted historically; people will understand it only when it is raised to a spiritual comprehension of the world. (page 224)

Moreover, academic researches acknowledge that next to nothing is verifiable about the life of Christ. In these lectures Steiner states:

> It must be understood that one cannot speak of the Christ impulse in the same way that people discuss ordinary history. Important theologians claim that it is foolish to speak of the Gospels as historically true in the ordinary sense, since everything they offer as historical proof that

Christ actually lived can be written on a few sheets of paper. Well-known theologians today thus admit that it is useless to study the Gospels as historical documents; there is no way to prove that they represent historical facts. This is considered self-evident today. According to these famous theologians, a couple of sheets of paper could contain all of the historical proof—the sort one would write as authentic documents about other historic personages. What this really means, however, is that even what is written on those few sheets of paper is not true in the ordinary historical sense. (page 224)

The point is that the reality of the life of Christ is largely inaccessible to a materialistic, historic approach and, consequently, all attempts in this direction are futile. A notable contemporary example of this problem—research with inadequate means—is found in the so-called Jesus Seminar. The Jesus Seminar is a group of independent scholars who meet regularly to study texts relating to the life of Jesus and decide what parts are historically verifiable. Over seventy scholars have participated in the meetings since its founding in 1985. The group resolves controversy by a voting system and, on that basis, makes pronouncements. The Jesus Seminar has amassed over 1500 sayings attributed to Jesus and 387 reports on him. Their review includes not just the four Gospels but also some eighteen lesser ones. They have decided that about eighteen percent of the sayings attributed to Jesus and sixteen percent of the stories about him are historically true. This puts their percentages higher than the scholars Steiner describes above. However, they reject the historical value of many of the most spiritually significant statements of Jesus Christ. For example, the "I am" sayings in the Gospel of St. John are not deemed historical. Quoting from the brief report by Gregory Jenks, here is what the Jesus Seminar makes of Jesus:

1. Jesus appears to have been an itinerant sage who delivered his parables and aphorisms in public and private venues for both friends and opponents in return for food and drink.
2. He never claimed to be (nor allowed others to call him) the Messiah or a divine being.
3. Jesus taught a wisdom that emphasized a simple trust in God's unstinting goodness and the generosity of others. Life was to be lived and celebrated without boundaries and without thought for the future. He rejected asceticism.
4. Ritual ceremonies had no value. Purity taboos and social barriers were never allowed to come between the people who responded to God and one another in simple trust.
5. There were no religious "brokers" in Jesus' vision of God's domain. No priests, no prophets, no messiahs. Not even Jesus himself was to be inserted between a person and God.
6. To experience forgiveness one simply had to offer forgiveness to others.
7. No theological beliefs served as a test for participation in God's domain.
8. Apocalyptic speculation with future punishments for the wicked and rewards for the virtuous played no part in Jesus' teaching.
9. Jesus was killed because he refused to compromise this radical vision of life as God's festival banquet. Those defending the status quo with its elaborate brokerage system for religious favors had to destroy him or lose their hold over others.
10. Following his death his closest friends (especially Mary Magdalene and Peter the Fisherman) found that they continued to experience him as the one who made God real to them. The resurrection stories express their conviction that Jesus had been taken beyond death into God's own life.[5]

---

5. "Being honest to Jesus…and with each other," *Focus* (monthly newspaper of the Anglican Diocese of Brisbane), November 1998. (Available on the Jesus Seminar website, http://religion.rutgers.edu/jseminar/).

For one who has an understanding of the Cosmic Christ, as can be acquired from Rudolf Steiner's published spiritual scientific research on Christianity, these ten points paint a totally pathetic picture. They contain absolutely no sense for the Christ, the solar being who incarnated into Jesus at the Baptism in the Jordan. Of course this is to be expected, as the scholars, using their voting system, have no doubt eliminated every statement found in the texts that would help one acquire some inkling of this deepest mystery of Earth evolution. The contrast between this pathetic picture and the magnificent image of Jesus Christ that emerges from spiritual scientific research makes clear what Steiner was getting at with his story of the discussion between a person who could read with one who could not regarding what was to be found on a printed page.

With scholars such as those of the Jesus Seminar, people who understand spiritual science will find no possibility of meaningful dialogue, as these scholars simply are unable to grasp what spiritual science is. They work with inadequate means, for the tools of material, historical research will never reveal the truth about the life of Jesus Christ.

***

Having, at least briefly, introduced the reader to certain hurdles that must be overcome if one wishes to approach these lectures with understanding, let us turn to a few observations about the contents. The first eight lectures, all delivered in 1910, constitute a world historic event of the greatest imaginable significance. Here Steiner travels about Europe speaking, for the first time, on the theme of the reappearance of Christ in the etheric as developed from his spiritual scientific research. He tells his audiences that the second coming of Christ is an event that will begin in the period 1930–1940 with a few people experiencing it and that it will come to more and more people over the next 2,500 years. In each talk he develops a broad historic perspective and context for this message and each new presentation contains nuances that distinguish it from the others. He stresses that Christ will never inhabit a physical body again. Christ inhabited a physical body from the time of the Baptism, when he entered the body of Jesus, until the crucifixion on Golgotha.[6] Never before and never again will He take on physical form. His second coming is in an etheric form.

The etheric body is something visible only to clairvoyant perception. In *An Outline of Esoteric Science,* Steiner explains that all living things—plants, animals, and humans—have a subtle etheric body that makes life possible. At the time of death, the etheric body separates from the physical body and the physical body decays following the laws of inorganic chemistry. The reason people will be able to perceive Christ in the etheric is that Christ endows them with what Steiner calls "the new natural clairvoyance." This new natural clairvoyance will become the possession of more and more people over the next two and half millennia. Through the fact that many people will possess this enhanced consciousness, human civilization will be completely transformed.

The ninth lecture presented in this volume was given in 1911 in Stuttgart, Germany and bears the title "The Etherization of the Blood." Here Steiner continues his spiritual scientific exploration of the working of the Christ in modern times. This research leads to the deepest insights into the nature of matter,

---

6. See for example, Rudolf Steiner, *According to St. Luke: The Gospel of Compassion and Love Revealed* (Anthroposophic Press, 2001; GA 114).

showing, in particular, how the Christ is working into the very material processes of man and the earth with a tremendous transformative power. The lecture also gives intimate details of how the Christ approaches human souls who are in deep need. They perceive him in His etheric body. His etheric body appears like a physical body but, because it vanishes, they realize it is not physical. Christ has the power to appear simultaneously to thousands of people all around the world. His etheric body is the only etheric body capable of working in the physical world as a physical body does. Here is how Steiner describes Christ appearing to a suffering individual or group:

Individuals may become aware that someone has suddenly approached to help them become alert to something. The truth is, Christ has come to them, although they believe that they see a physical man. They will come to realize, however, that this is a suprasensory being, since he will immediately vanish. Many will have this experience while sitting silently in a room, oppressed with a heavy heart and not knowing which way to turn. The door will open, and the etheric Christ will appear to console that person. The Christ will become a living comforter. Though it may seem strange now, it is nevertheless true that even large numbers of people will often be sitting together and wondering what to do, and they will see the etheric Christ. He will be there and confer with them; he will cast his word into such gatherings. (page 135–140)

Almost a century has passed since Rudolf Steiner spoke these prophetic words. One therefore can ask if evidence of such Christ experiences exits today. In fact there have been many reports from people who claim to have experienced Christ in our time. Two Swedish researchers published ads in the newspapers asking for people to send written descriptions of Christ experiences. They published the results in a book that, unfortunately, is not available in English.[7] An English compilation of personal Christ experiences is published under the title *I Am with You Always: True Stories of Encounters with Jesus.*[8]

There are also web sites devoted to posting personal experiences of meetings with Christ. The opening page of one of them states: "Visions of Jesus Christ, A Registry of Modern Reports from People Who Claim to Have Seen the Lord."[9] The registry contains a number of very interesting reports. Another site describes itself as follows: "Welcome to Visions of Jesus Christ.com. This site is a collection of Christ encounters I have collected from the Internet, personal e-mails and conversations."[10]

A review of this material reveals that a number of the encounters occur in vivid dreams. Another group of experiences occur as part of near death experiences. A third group occurs during ordinary waking consciousness. In these latter cases Christ appears to be in an earthly body that then disappears. This last group is quite consistent with Steiner's description from "The Etherization of the Blood," quoted above. In making this statement I do not suggest that all the accounts stem from actual meetings with the risen Christ. Of course account must always be taken of the possibility of illusions and hallucinations, and even fabrications. On the other hand there is no reason to dismiss all these reports as illegitimate.

The remaining four lectures of this volume are of a quite different character. This is due to their occurring in 1917, the

7. Gunnar Hillerdal and Berndt Gustafsson, *Wie erlebten Christus* (Pforte Verlag, 2002).

8. G. Scott Sparrow (Thomas More Publishing, 2003).

9. Available from http://petitecute.home.att.net/visions.htm.

10. Available from http://www.visionsofjesuschrist.com/.

third year of the First World War, which desolated Europe, leaving upward of thirty million people dead. While these lectures were all delivered in neutral Switzerland the tragic condition of mankind is reflected in the lectures. The first three lectures were delivered as a series in Dornach and the fourth was given in Bern.

The three Dornach lectures explore the most difficult issue of modern time: the mystery of evil. Steiner sketches in exacting detail how organized occult groups attempt to divert humanity's attention from Christ's reappearance in their pursuit of power. Steiner states that no one can have any influence on the sovereign will of Christ. But these opponents of Christ are trying to deflect people away from experiencing Christ, trying that is, to affect our ability to experience Him.

In the last lecture, given in Bern, Steiner introduces a very important distinction: the distinction between the world of nature and the world of destiny. He explains that into the orderly, natural, law-abiding events of nature, a completely different world penetrates, altering circumstances without ever violating the natural order. Suppose, he says, a man is going on a walk in the mountains. Suddenly, he hears a voice saying: Can't you just wait here a few minutes? You don't have to continue just now! The man heeds the unknown voice and a boulder hurdles over the place he would have been. The man inevitably would have been killed had he not followed the voice. No laws of nature have been violated but the world is a different place for the man and his circle of acquaintances. This, Steiner states, is the extreme version. The mundane version can be found in myriad events of life. How many times is one delayed leaving home by some seeming nuisance without realizing what was prevented as a consequence? Or, alternatively, someone is delayed at an airport and as a consequence meets someone who turns out to be important for her life. This realm of "chance" happenings and avoided happenings is a vast realm that plays into human life and around the laws of nature without ever violating them, and makes our biographies what they are. This is the realm of destiny over which Christ is the ruler.

When we grasp that humanity will awaken more and more to an awareness of Christ working as Lord of Karma and giving conscious, wide-awake council to people every day all around the globe then we can begin to glean the social impact that Christ's working into earthly evolution will take. Christ as councilor will not be limited to comforting suffering souls. His words will sound to statesman, businessmen and scientists, whose hearts are open, guiding their activities in the way of the healing and true moral world order of Earth evolution.

• Publisher's Note

The lectures in this volume were presented by Rudolf Steiner at various times. At the time of the earlier lectures (before 1915), he was still active in the German Section of the Theosophical Society and often used the terms *theosophy* and *theosophical* when referring to his own spiritual insights, which he later called *anthroposophy*, or *spiritual science*. In keeping with a suggestion from Rudolf Steiner, after the Anthroposophical Society was formed, the terms *theosophy* and *theosophical* generally have been replaced by *anthroposophy* or *spiritual science*, except for specific references to the theosophical movement.

I · The Appearance of Christ in the Etheric

Karlsruhe, January 25, 1910

Those who have concerned themselves for some time with spiritual science and its view of the world are affected by the various thoughts, ideas, and knowledge they have gained, and, as a result, numerous questions arise. Indeed, we develop as scientists of spirit by applying the ideas of spiritual science to these questions, which are really questions of sensation, feeling, and character—in other words, questions of life.

These ideas are not intended merely to satisfy theoretical or scientific curiosity; they illuminate the mysteries of life and existence. Such thoughts and ideas cannot become truly fruitful until we no longer merely think, feel, and sense their meaning and significance but, instead, are encouraged to look at the world about us in new ways. These ideas should fill us with warmth; they should become impulses within us—forces in our feeling and thinking. This will happen more and more as we obtain answers to certain questions and as these in turn present us with new questions. Thus we are led from questions to answers, the answers give rise to further questions, and so on. This is how we move forward in spiritual knowledge and in spiritual life.

It will be some time yet before it will be possible in public lectures to reveal the most intimate aspects of spiritual life to modern humanity, but the time is coming when we will be able to discuss such matters within our own groups. Again and again, new members of the Anthroposophical Society may be surprised and shocked by one thing or another, but we would never make any progress in our work if we do not begin to discuss the intimate issues of life from the depths of spiritual scientific research and knowledge. Consequently, we will once again bring before our souls some of the more intimate facts of spiritual knowledge, although it may lead to misunderstandings among those of you who have immersed yourselves in spiritual life for a relatively short time.

No doubt, a significant question arises if we give more than abstract consideration to the idea of reincarnation, or repeated earthly lives, and instead allow ourselves to thoughtfully contemplate this spiritual fact. The resulting answers about reincarnation provide valuable fruit for our lives, and these in turn will lead to fresh questions. We may, for example, wonder whether people live on earth more than one time. We may wonder whether we return again and again in new embodiments. And we might wish to ask about the deeper meaning of repeated lives. This is generally answered by saying that this is how we continually ascend; by experiencing the fruits of our earlier earthly lives in those that follow, we eventually perfect ourselves. But this is still a rather general, abstract opinion. We cannot fully understand the significance of repeated lives on earth unless we have a more exact knowledge of earthly life as a whole and its meaning.

If, for example, our earth were to remain unchanged—that is, if human beings kept returning to a place that remained essentially the same—then there would in fact be little to gain through successive incarnations. On the contrary, the real meaning of reincarnation lies in the fact that each earthly incarnation presents fresh fields of learning and experience. This is not as obvious over short periods, but if we survey long stretches of time (as we can through spiritual science), it becomes immediately obvious that each earthly epoch assumes a very different form and that we are continually faced with new experiences.

And we must understand something else; we must become aware of the changes that take place in the life of the earth itself. If we miss something that should have been experienced and learned during a particular epoch of our earthly evolution, then, even though we return to a new incarnation, we will have utterly failed to allow a necessary experience to flow into us during a preceding epoch. As a result we will be unable to use our forces and faculties in the right way during a later period.

In general, we can say that something is possible almost anywhere on earth during our time, something that was not possible during the previous incarnations of those who are now alive on earth. It seems strange, but this fact nevertheless has great significance. In the present incarnation, it is possible for a certain number of persons to come to spiritual science—that is, to take up the conclusions of today's spiritual research in the field of spiritual science. Naturally, it may be considered insignificant that a few people come together and allow the discoveries of spiritual research to flow into them. Those who find this unimportant, however, do not understand the significance of reincarnation and the fact that an individual can take up something only during one particular incarnation. And if one fails to take it up, it will be missed entirely and something will be lacking in following incarnations. Above all, we must impress upon our minds the fact that what we learn today through spiritual science unites with our souls, and we bring this with us when we descend to our next incarnation.

Today we will try to understand what this means for our souls. Therefore, we must connect much that you already know from other lectures and from your reading with numerous spiritual facts that may be new to you. First, let us return to earlier periods in the evolution of humanity. We have often looked back to earlier periods of our earthly evolution, and it has been said that we now live in the fifth period after the great Atlantean catastrophe. This fifth period was preceded by the fourth, Greek and Latin period, during which those peoples indicated the principle ideas and feelings of earthly volition. This, in turn, was preceded by the third period, that of the Egyptians, Chaldeans, Babylonian, and Assyrians. And this was preceded by the ancient Persian period, which followed the ancient Indian period.

If we delve even further into antiquity, we come to the great Atlantean catastrophe that destroyed an ancient continent, the ancient mainland Atlantis, which once extended into the area of today's Atlantic Ocean. That cataclysm gradually engulfed the continent and thereby gave our solid earth its present countenance. Then, continuing back, we come to even earlier periods, before the Atlantean catastrophe; we find civilizations and conditions of life that developed on the Atlantean continent— the civilizations of the Atlantean races. Even earlier conditions preceded these.

Consider what history tells us—and, indeed, it does not go back very far. We can easily be led to believe that things on earth have always appeared as they do now, although such a belief is entirely unfounded, even in relation to shorter periods of time. But this is not the case. On the contrary, conditions on earth have altered fundamentally, and the soul conditions of human beings have also changed tremendously. The souls of those sitting here today incarnated during each of these ancient periods, always in bodies that were in keeping with the various epochs, and they absorbed what was needed during these periods of earthly evolution. With each succeeding incarnation, the soul developed new faculties. Our souls were entirely different from what they are today—perhaps not so noticeably different during the Greco-Latin era, but during the old Persian period they differed greatly from those of today, and even more so during the ancient Indian period. In those ancient periods, our souls were endowed with very different faculties and lived through entirely different conditions.

Today, therefore, we will more clearly understand each other if we call before our mind's eye, as distinctly as possible, the nature of our souls, say, in the age after the Atlantean catastrophe (thus we will be dealing with a period of great significance). Our souls were incarnated in bodies that were appropriate only to life on earth during the first Indian civilization. We must not see this Indian civilization as having been significant only in India. The Indian people at that time were merely the most advanced and most important, but the civilization of the whole earth derived its characteristic qualities from what the leaders indicated to those ancient Indians.

Consider our souls as they were at that time. First we must say that the kind of knowledge we have today was completely impossible then. At that time, there was no clearly defined self-awareness, or "I consciousness." The concept of "I" hardly occurred to human beings then. To be sure, the I existed as a force in human beings, but *knowledge* of the I is different from the force and effect of the I. Human beings were not yet endowed with the sort of intimate inner life that we have today. They possessed entirely different faculties—for example, what we have often called an ancient, vague clairvoyance.

When we consider the nature of the human soul during the day, at that time, we find it did not actually experience itself an I; instead, people experienced themselves as members of a tribe or race. Just as one's hand is a part of one's body, likewise the separate I, as a member of the community formed by the tribe, represented the people. The individual did not yet perceive an individual I, as one does today; it was the tribal I on which one's attention was fixed. People thus lived through the day without a clear understanding that they were individual human beings. When evening came, however, one passed into sleep, but consciousness did not become totally darkened as it does today. Instead, during sleep the soul was able to perceive spiritual realities. Dreams today are mere shadows of what was normal then, when people perceived surrounding spiritual events and facts in their dreams—realities that, as a rule, today's dreams no longer represent. These were the perceptions of people at that time, and thus they had an awareness of the spiritual world. It was a reality to them—not through any sort of logic or proof, but simply because each night they found themselves in the spiritual world, though only with a vague and dreamy awareness.

But this was not their most their essential quality. Aside from the conditions of being asleep and awake, there were in-between states during which they were neither completely asleep nor wholly awake. At such times, their I consciousness was less acute than it was during the day, but on the other hand their perception of spiritual events in dreamy clairvoyance was substantially stronger than during the night. So, whereas there were certainly intermediate states in which people lacked self-awareness, they were, nevertheless, endowed with clairvoyance. In such states, people were in a kind of trance, and I consciousness was dimmed. They were unaware of being a human individual, but they clearly saw themselves as members of the spiritual world, where they could perceive and be certain of its existence. These were the experiences of the human souls of the ancient Indian period, and this conscious life in the spiritual world was even clearer during the earlier period of Atlantis—very much clearer. When we consider this, therefore, we look back to an ancient era of dim, vague clairvoyance in our souls, which diminished gradually during human evolution.

If we had remained at that stage of ancient, dreamy clairvoyance, we could never have acquired the individual I awareness we have today. We could never have realized that we are human individuals. We had to lose that awareness of the spiritual world in exchange for I consciousness. In the future, we shall have both. While maintaining our I consciousness, we will all regain what amounts to full clairvoyance. Today this is possible only for those who have traveled the path of initiation. In the future, everyone will once again be able to look into the spiritual world, and yet we will experience ourselves as human beings—as I beings.

Imagine again what has taken place. The soul has passed from incarnation to incarnation. Initially, the soul was clairvoyant. Later, the increasing awareness of self grew continually more distinct, and with it came the possibility of forming one's own judgments. As long as we look clairvoyantly into the spiritual world and do not experience ourselves as I beings, judgments—the ability to combine thoughts—remain impossible.

Logical thinking emerged gradually in exchange for the old clairvoyance, which diminished with each succeeding incarnation. People lived less and less in those states in which they could look into the spiritual world. Instead, they adjusted to the physical plane, cultivated logical thinking, and experienced themselves as individuals, and clairvoyance gradually receded.

Human beings now perceive the external world and become increasingly entangled in it, but real connection with the spiritual world becomes more tenuous. We can therefore say that, in the distant past, people were really spiritual beings, because they associated directly with other spirit beings as their "companions." They felt that they belonged with other spiritual beings, whom people can no longer perceive today with ordinary human senses. As we know, beyond the world that surrounds us today, there are also other spiritual worlds inhabited by other spiritual beings, but people today cannot look into those worlds with ordinary consciousness. Earlier, however, people dwelled in them, both while asleep at night and during the intermediate state we mentioned. People then lived in the spiritual world and interacted with these other beings. People can no longer do this under normal conditions. Human beings have, as it were, been cast out of their home, the spiritual world, and with each new incarnation humankind becomes more and more firmly established in this earthly world below.

When you consider these facts, bear in mind that we cannot learn to speak and think today unless we grow up among human beings, because these faculties can be acquired only among other human beings. If a child were cast away on some lonely island to grow up without associating with other human beings, the faculties of thinking and speaking would not develop. So we can see that the development of any being is determined (in part, at least) by the sort of entities that being grows up among. Evolution is affected by this fact. You can see this among animals. It is known that if dogs are unable to meet or associate with human beings, they forget how to bark. As a rule, the descendants of such dogs are unable to bark at all. It is important whether a being grows up and lives among one kind of being or another.

You can see, therefore, that it does make a difference whether you live on the physical plane among human beings today, or whether you (as the same soul, so to speak) lived earlier among spirit beings in a spiritual world that can no longer be observed by ordinary sight. During that earlier time, the soul developed in a different way; human beings had different impulses than they did while living among the gods. They developed one sort of impulse among humankind, and another among the gods. In spiritual sanctuaries and among scientists and others who still knew of such matters, people understood that our incarnations passed through these various earthly periods. They looked back to an ancient period—even before the Atlantean catastrophe—when human beings lived in direct contact with the gods, or spirits, and naturally sensed and experienced the world in an completely different way. You can imagine that the human soul must have experienced very different sensations in an age when it knew for certain that it could look up to higher beings and recognize itself as a member of that higher world. Consequently, the human soul learned to feel and sense in an entirely different way.

Higher knowledge has always known this; such knowledge has always looked back to that time when human beings were in direct contact with divine spiritual beings, which meant that the soul felt itself part the divine spiritual world. But this also engendered soul forces and impulses that were spiritual in a totally different sense than those of today. At that time, while the soul still experienced itself as part of the higher world, the volition that spoke from this soul also came from the divine spiritual world. One could say that this volition was inspired, because the soul dwelt among the gods. This period—when humankind was still united with the divine spiritual beings—is spoken of in the ancient wisdom as the Golden Age, or Krita Yuga. We must look back to a time preceding the Atlantean catastrophe to find the greater part of this age.

Afterward, there was a time when human beings no longer experienced a connection with the spiritual world as they did during Krita Yuga; their impulses felt less determined by their association with the gods, and even their ability to see the spirit world grew dimmer. However, they retained the memory of having lived with spirits and gods, and this was especially distinct in the ancient Indian world. There they spoke easily of spiritual matters; they could point to the world of physical perception and yet recognize maya, or illusion, there. This was because human beings retained physical perceptions for only a relatively short time.

That was the situation in ancient India. The souls in ancient India no longer saw the gods, but they still saw spiritual realities and lower spirit beings. Higher spirit beings were still visible to a few, but a living association with the gods was obscured even to them. Volitional impulses from the divine spiritual realm had disappeared, but it was still possible to glimpse spiritual realities during particular states of consciousness—during sleep and during the intermediate state mentioned. The most important realities of the spirit world, however, which had previously been a matter of experience, had become merely a sort of "knowledge" of the truth—something the soul still knew but had only the *effect* of knowledge, or truth. Certainly, human beings were still in the spiritual world, but their assurance of it was not as strong during this later time as it had been. This period is known as the Silver Age, or Treta Yuga.

Following this came the period of the incarnations in which human vision was increasingly cut off from the spirit world. Instead, it adjusted more and more to the immediate outer world of the senses and, accordingly, became more firmly entrenched in the world of the senses. This period, during which human I consciousness emerged, is known as the Bronze Age, or Dvapara Yuga. Although human beings no longer had the lofty, direct spiritual knowledge of earlier periods, at least something of the spiritual world remained in humanity as a whole. One could describe this by comparing it to modern human beings, who, as they grow older, retain some of the joy of youth. The joy itself has indeed fled, but having had that experience, it is known, and one can speak of it with familiarity. Similarly, the souls of that time were still somewhat familiar with the way to spirit worlds. This is the essential feature of Dvapara Yuga.

During the following period, even this familiarity with the spiritual world ended, and the doors of the spiritual world were closed. Human vision became so confined to the world of the senses and to intellectual elaborations of those impressions that humankind could only reflect upon the spiritual world. This is the lowest means of knowing the spiritual world. Indeed, what human beings now knew from experience was only the physical, sensory world. If they wished to know something of the spirit world, they had to employ reflection. This is the period when humankind became the least spiritual and, accordingly, the most attached to and rooted in the world of the senses. This was necessary so that self-awareness would gradually reach the peak of its evolution, for only through the sturdy opposition of the outer world could human beings begin to distinguish themselves from the world and experience themselves as individual beings. This last period is called Kali Yuga, meaning the dark age.

I would like to point out that these terms can also be applied to more extensive epochs. Krita Yuga, for example, may refer to a much broader period, because even before the Golden Age existed, human beings participated in and experienced still higher spheres. Hence, much earlier periods might be included in the term "Golden Age." If we are moderate, however, in our claims—if we are content with the measure of spiritual experience just described—it is possible to divide past events in this way. Definite periods of time can be assigned to all such eras. To be sure, evolution moves forward slowly, through gradual stages, but there are certain boundaries that allow us to say such a thing was primarily true before, and, later, another condition of life and consciousness prevailed. Accordingly, we must say that, in the sense of our first use of the term, Kali Yuga began around 3101 B.C. We therefore see that our souls have appeared repeatedly on earth in new incarnations, during which human vision has become increasingly shut off from the spirit world, while becoming more and more limited to the external world of the senses. We see that, with each new incarnation, our souls enter new conditions in which something new can always be learned. What we can gain from Kali Yuga is the possibility of becoming firmly established in I consciousness. This was impossible previously, because the human being first had to absorb the I.

If souls neglect what an incarnation within a particular epoch has to offer, it is very difficult to make up for the loss in a later epoch. They must wait a very long time for the possibility of making good on the loss in a particular way, and we must certainly not depend on getting that chance. Let us therefore recall that something essential occurred at the point in time when the doors to the spiritual world were shut tight. That was the period during which John the Baptist was active, as well as the Christ. This time had already seen the passing of 3,100 years of the Kali Yuga, and it was essential that people had incarnated at least once or twice during this age—ideally, several times. Self-awareness had become firmly established, and memory of the spiritual world had evaporated; if human beings did not wish to lose all connection with the spirit world, they had to learn how to experience spirit within the I. They had to develop the self in such a way that this I—its inner being— could at least be certain of a spirit world, that humankind belongs to it, and that there are higher spirit beings. The I had to make itself capable of inwardly experiencing and believing in the spiritual world.

If, during the time of Jesus Christ, someone had expressed the truth of that period, it might have been said that, once upon a time, human beings were able to experience the kingdom of heaven outside of their I, in the spiritual distances they attained when they emerged from their lower selves. Previously, human beings had to experience the kingdom of heaven, the spiritual world, far from the I. At that time, however, the kingdom of heaven could not be experienced in this way; human beings had changed so much that the I now had to experience the kingdom of heaven within. The kingdom of heaven approached humankind to the extent that it worked into the I.

John the Baptist proclaimed this to humanity by saying, "The kingdom of heaven is at hand"—that is, it approaches the I. Previously, it was to be found outside of the human being, but now it had to be embraced within the very core of one's being—the I, a kingdom of heaven now come near.

During this Kali Yuga, precisely because human beings could no longer leave the world of the senses and enter the spiritual world, the divine Christ being entered the physical world of the senses. This is why the Christ had to descend into a man of flesh, Jesus of Nazareth. By witnessing the life and activities of the Christ on the physical earth, human beings in physical bodies could regain their connection to the kingdom of heaven, the spiritual world. The time when the Christ walked the earth thus fell in the Kali Yuga—a time when those who comprehended their age and did not live in a dull and unenlightened way might recognize that it was necessary for God to descend among human beings, so that their lost connection with the spiritual world could be regained.

If no one at that time had been able to understand this and establish an active soul connection with the Christ, all human connection with the spiritual world would have gradually been lost, and human beings would not have received a connection with the kingdom of heaven into the I. If everyone living at that crucial time had persisted in darkness, this significant event might have passed by unnoticed. Human souls, then, would have become withered, desolate, and depraved. Certainly, they would have continued to incarnate for awhile without the Christ, but they could never have planted in the I what was needed to regain their connection with the kingdom of heaven. The appearance of Christ on earth might have been overlooked by everyone, just as it passed unnoticed, for example, by the inhabitants of Rome. Among these, it was said, "Somewhere, in a dingy side street, there lives a strange sect of horrid people, and among them there is a detestable spirit who calls himself Jesus of Nazareth, and who preaches to the people, inciting them to all kinds of heinous acts." That is how much they knew of Christ in Rome at a certain period. You may also be aware that it was the great Roman historian Tacitus who described the Christ in a similar way about a hundred years after those events in Palestine.

Indeed, it is true; not everyone realized that something of the greatest importance was taking place—an event that, striking divine light into unearthly darkness, was able to carry human beings through Kali Yuga. Humankind was given the possibility of further evolution, because there were certain souls who comprehended that moment in time; they knew the meaning behind the fact that the Christ was walking the earth.

Imagine that you are, for a moment, in that time. You could easily say, "Yes, it would be very possible to live then and still know nothing of the appearance of Jesus Christ in the physical world. It would be possible to live on earth without taking this significant event into one's consciousness." Could it, then, also be possible that something of infinite importance is taking place today, and that human beings are not taking it into their consciousness? Could it be that something tremendously important is taking place in the world, right now, of which our own contemporaries have no idea? This is indeed the case. Something extremely important is happening, but it is perceptible only to spiritual vision. There is a great deal of talk about "periods of transition." We are indeed living in one, and it is momentous. The important thing is that we are living right at the end of the Dark Age, and a new epoch is just beginning in which human beings will gradually develop new faculties and human souls will gradually go through a change.

It is hardly a wonder that most people are not the least aware of this, considering that most people also failed to notice the Christ event at the beginning of our era. Kali Yuga came to an end in 1899; now we must adapt to a new age. What is beginning will slowly prepare humankind for new soul faculties.

The first signs of these new soul faculties will soon begin to appear in a few isolated souls. Those signs will become clearer during the fourth decade, between 1930 and 1940, and especially in 1933, 1935, and 1937. Faculties that are still rare in people will begin to manifest as natural abilities. Along with this, there will be great changes, and biblical prophecies will be fulfilled. Everything will be transformed for those on earth, as well as for those who are no longer in a physical body. Regardless of where they are, souls are meeting entirely new faculties. Everything is changing, but the most significant event of our time is a deep, decisive transformation in human soul faculties.

Kali Yuga has run its course, and human souls are beginning to develop new faculties, since this is precisely the purpose of the new age. These new faculties will cause souls to exhibit seemingly spontaneous clairvoyant powers, which had to remain in the subconscious during Kali Yuga. A number of souls will have the unique experience of self-awareness, along with the feeling of living in another world—a world entirely different from the one of ordinary consciousness. It will be like a kind of shadowy, vague presentiment, similar to the gift of sight to one born blind. Through esoteric training, as we call it, clairvoyant faculties will be acquired much more readily, but because humankind continues to evolve, these will also appear naturally—at least in rudimentary form.

During our epoch, it is more likely than ever before that people will be unable to comprehend this most important event for humanity. People might fail to understand that it provides a real glimpse into the spiritual world, though only a shadowy and vague one. There might be so much evil and materialism on earth, for example, that most of humanity would not show any understanding and, instead, see clairvoyants as mad and place them into insane asylums with those whose souls have developed in a muddled way. This epoch could pass by unnoticed, as it were. Nevertheless, we are sending out the message today; just as John the Baptist, the forerunner of Christ, and Christ himself once announced: A new age is at hand, and human souls must take a step upward toward the kingdom of heaven.

This great event might easily pass by without human understanding. It would not disprove what we have said if, between 1930 and 1940, materialistic people were to triumph and say, "Yes, there have been a lot of fools, but no indication of the great events that were predicted." Nevertheless, it would be a great misfortune if materialists were to triumph and humanity were to overlook these events. Even if people prove unable to perceive this great event, it will nonetheless take place.

The event we are discussing is the human acquisition of a new faculty of perception in the etheric realm. This will involve a limited number of people at first, followed gradually by others. Humankind will have 2,500 years in which to evolve and increase these faculties. People must not miss the opportunity offered in this period. To let it pass by would be a great misfortune; humanity would have to wait to finally develop this faculty and make up the loss. This capacity will enable people to see something of the etheric world in their surroundings, which until now has been generally imperceptible. People today see only the physical human body; in the future, however, they will also be able to see the etheric body, at least as a shadowy image. People will also be able to experience a relationship to the deeper events in the etheric world. They will experience images and presentiments of events in the spiritual world and find that such events also happen on the physical plane after three or four days. They will see certain things in etheric images and know that, within the next few days, something specific will occur.

These transformations will come about in human soul capacities, resulting in what may be described as etheric vision. And who is connected with this? The being we call the Christ, who appeared in the flesh on earth at the beginning of our era. He will never appear again in a physical body; that was a unique event. Christ will return in an etheric form, however, during the time we have been discussing. People will then learn to perceive the Christ, because through etheric vision they will grow upward toward the one who will enter an etheric body, but never again a physical body. It will be necessary for human beings to grow toward perceiving the Christ, for he truly said, "I am with you always, even unto the end of the earth." He is here; he is in our spiritual world, and those who are blessed can perceive his presence in the etheric realm.

The Apostle Paul was convinced by this kind of perception in the event near Damascus. This same etheric vision will be cultivated individually as a natural faculty by people. An event like Paul's will become increasingly possible for human beings in the coming period.

It will then no longer be necessary to prove the existence of Christ through all sorts of documents, because eyewitnesses will experience the presence of the living Christ in his etheric body. Through this experience, people will realize that this is the Christ, the being who consummated the Mystery of Golgotha at the beginning of our era. Just as Paul was convinced of Christ's presence near Damascus, because of their experiences in the etheric realm, people will be convinced that Christ truly lives. Consequently, we comprehend spiritual science in a completely different way. We learn that it presents us with a tremendous responsibility, because it is a preparation for the very real reappearance of the Christ. He will reappear, because human beings will be rising toward him in etheric vision. Once we understand this, we will see that spiritual science prepares human beings for the return of Christ, so that they will not have the misfortune of missing this great event but be prepared to seize the great moment of Christ's second coming. Human beings will be able to see etheric bodies, and among these etheric bodies people will be able to see the etheric body of Christ; humankind will grow into a world where the Christ will be visible to newly awakened faculties.

The greatest mystery of our time concerns the second coming of Christ, which assumes its true form as I have described. Materialistic minds will, in a certain sense, usurp this event. What has just been said—that all true spiritual knowledge points to this time—will be proclaimed often during the coming years. But today's materialistic minds corrupt everything, and so this type of mentality will be unable to imagine that human souls must advance to etheric vision and to Christ in an etheric body.

Materialistic minds will claim this event as another descent of Christ into the flesh—a physical incarnation. Some, in their colossal conceit, will turn this event to their own advantage by claiming that they are the reincarnated Christ. Consequently, the coming period may bring false Christs. Anthroposophists, however, should be so prepared for spiritual life that they will not confuse the second coming of Christ in a spiritual body—which is perceptible only to a higher vision—with such a physical reappearance. That will be one of the most dangerous temptations to assail humanity. Helping to overcome this temptation will be the task of those who learn to raise themselves to a comprehension of the spirit through spiritual science—those who, instead of dragging spirit down into matter, wish to ascend into the spirit world. Consequently, we must speak of the second coming of Christ in this way—that we must lift ourselves to Christ in the spiritual world by acquiring etheric vision.

The Christ is always present, but in the spiritual world; we can reach him if we rise into that world. Anthroposophic teaching should be transformed within us as a strong desire to prevent this event from passing by unnoticed. Rather, in the time remaining, we must gradually educate humanity to cultivate these new faculties and thereby reunite with the Christ. Otherwise, humanity would have to wait a long time for another opportunity—indeed, until the next incarnation of earth itself. If humanity were to ignore the return of Christ, the vision of Christ in the etheric body would be limited to those who, through esoteric training, are ready to rise to that experience. It would be a long time before humanity would again have an opportunity to acquire these capacities and before this great event could be understood by humankind through naturally developed faculties.

We see that there is, in fact, something in our time that justifies the active presence of spiritual science in the world. Its purpose is not to satisfy scientific curiosity or people's need for theories. Spiritual science prepares people for this event by understanding this period with clear cognition, seeing what is truly present and the fact that it may go by without being brought to fruition. This is the aim of spiritual science.

It will be most important to grasp the event of Christ's reappearance, because other events will follow. Other events preceded the event of Christ in Palestine; similarly, after Christ has become visible in the etheric body, those who predicted his appearance will become his successors. All those who prepared the way for him will be recognized in a new way by those who have experienced the new Christ event. Those who lived at one time on earth as Moses, Abraham, and other prophets will again be recognizable to human beings. We will realize that, even as Abraham preceded Christ and prepared his way, Abraham also assumed the task of helping later on with the work of Christ. Those who are awake and do not sleep through the greatest event of the near future will gradually unite with all those who preceded the Christ event as patriarchs. Then will come the reappearance of the great host of those toward whom we will be able rise. The one who led humanity's descent into the physical plane will reappear after Christ and lead humanity upward to reunite with the spirit worlds.

Looking back at very early human evolution, we see that there was a moment after which we may say that humanity descended even further from fellowship with the spirit world and sank more and more into the material world. Although the image that follows has a material side, it will be useful here.

At one time, human beings were companions of spirit beings; human spirit lived in the spirit world and, because of this, human beings were called "sons of the gods." Their continually reincarnating souls, however, participated more and more in the phenomenal world. These sons of the gods in humankind took delight in the "daughters of the earth"—those souls who had sympathy for the physical world. This means that the human spirit—previously permeated by divine spirit—sank into the physical world of the senses. Human spirit mated with the intellect, which is bound to the brain and entangled in the sensory realm. This spirit must now find the path along which it descended, and by climbing it become again a son of the gods. This spirit is now a "son of humanity," and it would perish here in the physical world unless it ascends, as a son of humanity, to the divine beings and to the light of the spirit world. In the future this spirit will find delight in the "daughters of the gods." It was necessary for human evolution that the sons of gods unite with the daughters of the earth—the souls fettered to the physical world—so that, as sons of humanity, human beings could master the physical plane. But it will be necessary for human beings in the future (as sons of humanity) to find delight in the daughters of the gods—the divine spiritual light of wisdom, with which humankind must unite and again rise to the world of the gods.

Human volition will be fired by divine wisdom, and the most powerful impetus in this direction will be a vision of the sublime etheric figure of Jesus Christ by those who are prepared. The second coming of the Christ will be, for those who have naturally developed clairvoyance, just as the etheric Christ appeared to Paul. He will reappear to humankind once people realize that these faculties, which will come through the soul's evolution, are for this very purpose.

Let us use spiritual science so that it may serve not merely to satisfy our curiosity, but in such a way that it prepares us for the great missions of the human race, toward which we must continue to mature.

* * *

Rudolf Steiner's Answers to Questions following the Lecture

When we discuss and illuminate the more intimate mysteries as we have today, let's not regard them thoughtlessly in the typical manner of today; let us be very clear that anthroposophy should never become mere abstract theory. Of course, the teaching must be there; how could one rise to the sort of thoughts revealed here today if they could not be absorbed through teaching? It is essential, however, that it does not remain a teaching; it must be reshaped within our hearts into qualities of feeling, and it should make us into very different human beings. It should guide us toward the right use of our time on earth, so that during life we are changed entirely.

By trying not to say too much or too little, I have referred only briefly to important subjects. What was said, however, is significant not only for those who will be physically incarnated between 1930 and 1940, but also for those who will be in the spirit world, between death and a new birth. We must realize that souls in the spirit world influence the world of the living, although those on the physical plane may be quite unaware of this. As a result of the new Christ event, however, the relationship between those who are embodied on the physical plane and those who are in the spirit world will become increasingly conscious. Cooperation between physically embodied human beings and spirit beings will become possible. This should have been implied in our visualization of the prophets' reappearance to human beings on earth.

Therefore, you must imagine that, when these great moments arrive in the future, human beings will work together more consciously in both the physical and the spirit worlds. Today this is not possible, because we lack a common language. People here in the physical world use words that describe only physical phenomena and conditions. Between death and a new birth, however, human beings live in a world that is very different from the one we see around us, and they speak a different language. Out of all that is said in our world, those who have died can receive only what is spoken in spiritual science. Thus, in anthroposophy we are concerned with matters that will be increasingly understood by those who have died; what we say in this way benefits those between death and a new birth.

Humanity is preparing for a time when the influences of the spirit world will be felt more widely. The great events of the coming period will be discernible in all worlds. Even those who are between death and a new birth will have new experiences in that world as a result of the new Christ event in the etheric realm. Unless they have readied themselves on earth, however, they will not be able to understand these events any better than those now incarnated on earth; they must be properly prepared to receive the events of this important moment. It is essential for all souls now incarnated (whether or not they will still be physically embodied then) to prepare for these coming significant events by taking up anthroposophical truths. If they fail to do this, they will have to wait. If their earthly consciousness has not received the fruits of spiritual science, they will have to wait until another incarnation for the possibility of receiving the necessary teachings here on earth. Some things can be learned or experienced only on earth. One could say, for example, that in the spirit world it is impossible to gain any knowledge of death and that God had to descend to the physical world to die. In no other world can one learn the true nature of the Mystery of Golgotha as one can in the physical world. We have been led into the physical world to acquire what can be acquired only here. The Christ descended among humankind, because only here in the physical world could he demonstrate, through experience, something in the Mystery of Golgotha that would bear fruit in the spirit world. The seeds, however, must be sown here in the physical world.

2 · Spiritual Science and Etheric Vision

Heidelberg, January 27, 1910

The lectures at our group meetings would do little for our development if we could not speak occasionally about the more intimate processes of human spiritual life. In our groups, we should work toward attaining higher spiritual truths. Nevertheless, we must not imagine that such work involves learning mere theories or ideas. We prepare to receive higher truths through a certain feeling or sensation in our souls. By meeting each week in our groups, our souls should gradually mature to become receptive even to the elements of spiritual science that descend (or, if you prefer, ascend) from the more general truths that we can communicate in exoteric lectures to the general public—in other words, the concrete facts of life. Therefore, let us dedicate this evening in particular to this soul preparation.

There are certain things that should be presented to our souls—matters we will understand only gradually at first. Nevertheless, we can begin to get a sense of this if we mature enough through our groups. It must be assumed in this case that such truths will be received, with corresponding sensitivity, as a priceless treasure of soul, not as something that could be placed before an unprepared audience. We will ascend in our considerations gradually, from the known to the unknown.

A question arises, even in the minds of those familiar with the anthroposophic worldview: Do repeated human lives on earth serve any real purpose? One may accept the abstract truth of reincarnation, but abstract truth cannot really help us in life. Truths acquire meaning in life only when they can be transformed in our souls as a warm feeling, as a light that shines from within us and encourages us along life's path. This is why the abstract truth of reincarnation will not have meaning for us unless we know something more exact and intimate about the reason for successive human incarnations. This will be one of the questions that will occupy us here.

The other question is this: What exactly is the significance of the fact that, during our present incarnation, we are able to absorb anthroposophy into our souls, binding anthroposophic truths with our innermost life? We shall see that today these two matters will unite harmoniously.

You have often heard that two successive human incarnations do not follow in an arbitrary way; rather, once human beings have passed through death and out of one earthly life, they return to a new earthly life only when it provides the opportunity to learn something new that can be united with the soul. Naturally, this can be understood only by those who do not limit their study of earthly evolution to a few centuries or millennia. Only those who survey the whole evolution of the earth are able to comprehend things properly. In terms of physical phenomena, we learn, even from exoteric sources, that the very countenance of the earth has changed during relatively short periods of time.

If, for example, you read a description of the areas we now inhabit and see how they might have looked when Christ walked the earth, you will find the whole appearance of this region changed during a relatively few centuries. You might wonder how much change has take place in the moral and social conditions of civilization during the course of those centuries. Try to imagine for a moment what children used to learn at the beginning of our era and what they learn today; try to imagine this, and then recall what you have learned from anthroposophic teachings—that we can look back to a remote past when the earth presented an entirely different appearance. For the most part, today's continents did not yet exist; there was, however, an immense continent in the place now occupied today by the Atlantic Ocean. Imagine all that must have occurred throughout those long periods that changed the appearance of the earth to what it is today.

If you bring all of this before your souls, you must admit that it is possible for souls to experience something new in each earthly existence, always receiving new fruits and uniting them with their lives for the passage through the spirit worlds between dying and a new birth. Souls return to a new incarnation when the conditions have changed enough so that something new can be learned, making it worthwhile to descend again to a new earthly life.

It is not just an arbitrary play of forces and beings behind the phenomenal world that brings us down again and again into new incarnations; every incarnation contributes a new force and faculty, a new member in the divine plan of human life as a whole. Unless we look at life in this way, the law of repeated lives on earth has no real meaning. We must also ask ourselves whether it is possible to miss an opportunity. Is there something that depends on whether we make the most of every incarnation in the right way? If it were simply a matter of repeating our present life in the next incarnation, it could be argued that there is plenty of time, since we'll be back many, many more times.

If we consider the most important facts of life, however, and understand that the earth can give us something during one period of time that cannot be experienced again during another, we come to realize that it is indeed possible to miss opportunities. We can thus acquire an inner sense of responsibility to make the best use of each earthly embodiment in the right way. When we take a quick look backward with the help that spiritual investigation offers, we come to a more precise idea of how we can use these incarnations.

There are certain facts that are already familiar to you, but I will extend them to include something unknown to most of you. What you already know is that, during our earliest incarnations, our souls possessed entirely different faculties than they do today. The faculties by which modern humanity lives and works did not always exist. What is especially active in the human soul today? It is the capacity to receive the external realities of the world in an exact way through the senses. Humankind possesses self-awareness and the power to reason, which we can apply to sensory perception, thus combining what we receive through the senses. In this way, human beings gain an image of the world through cognition. We know, however, that if people develop their souls further through the methods described in my book *How to Know Higher Worlds*, they begin to be able to perceive a surrounding spiritual environment.[1]

---

1. *How to Know Higher Worlds: The Classic Guide to the Spiritual Journey* (Anthroposophic Press, 2002; GA 10).

We know that there is a spiritual eye that can be opened, and that we can awaken higher, suprasensory faculties, which are dormant in the average person today. We know that there was a time when every human being could perceive the spiritual world, but we know also that there will be a time when the spiritual world will again be able to flow into our souls, just as light and color flow into the eyes of one who was blind, but to whom sight was restored. Light and color existed all along, but they were blocked by organs incapable of receiving them. Today, humanity can look into the spiritual world only as the result of an abnormal kind of development or by following special methods of self-development. The normal condition today provides the ability to perceive worldly phenomena through the outer senses and to combine those perceptions through reason, or intellect, which is connected with the physical brain.

Human beings, however, have not always been what they are today. If we have opened our clairvoyant vision to the body of facts called the akashic record, we can look back to a remote period in human evolution and find that normal human soul faculties were entirely different then.[2] In ancient times, all human beings had a kind of clairvoyance—not the kind one can acquire today using methods of initiation, but an entirely different sort of clairvoyance. We must describe it as a vague, dreamy clairvoyance. Such clairvoyance accompanied certain abnormal conditions and arose on its own; it was not necessary to use special methods. We would have to go back to the very remote past, certainly, if we wanted to find human beings endowed with consistent clairvoyance, but even then it

2. *Akasha* is the primordial substance of space, the "etheric," which contains the memory of the cosmos, or akashic record. See, for example, Rudolf Steiner, *The Fifth Gospel: From the Akashic Record* (Rudolf Steiner Press, 2001; GA 148).

occurred only during certain transitional states such as the shift from sleeping to awaking. The further we go back, the more we find this form of clairvoyance.

You will recall that, going back through the various periods of civilization, we come to particular epochs of human culture. We are now living in a period of civilization that was preceded by one designated the Greco-Latin epoch. This was preceded by another period, named for its leading nations, the Egypto-Chaldean epoch. This was preceded by the one we call the ancient Persian epoch. Still further back, we come to what we call ancient India, a civilization that only the clairvoyant eye can see. The period that produced the Vedas arose much later as a weak echo of the sublime wisdom given to the world by the Seven Holy Rishis during that earliest primeval Indian civilization. If we go back even further, we see the great Atlantean catastrophe that transformed the appearance of our earth through cataclysms of water and fire, so that the Atlantean continent gradually disappeared. In its place, the locations of today's Africa and Europe arose on one side, and that of America on the other. We could go even further back, and the akashic record shows that those who lived on that ancient Atlantean continent possessed soul faculties that were entirely different from ours—faculties that seem unbelievable to modern humankind, because they are so remote from anything people know today.

Our own souls existed throughout those various periods; they existed in different bodies, and each time they possessed different faculties. If we could look back, we should find that our souls were endowed with clairvoyant receptivity. Especially during the transitional states between sleeping and awaking, they witnessed the spirit world. At that time, you would see that you could perceive for yourselves the beings and processes of the spirit worlds. In those days, there was no possibility that human souls would be tempted to deny the existence of the spirit world, because they could see it; they were directed toward the physical world only for a few hours during the day. The phenomena of the external world were not yet arranged visibly as they were in later periods. Hence, when human beings were in the transitional state between sleeping and awaking, they were surrounded by a world that they experienced as spiritual, and it convinced them that it was the world from which humankind originated. Humankind descended from the spirit world because they needed something that could be acquired only in the physical world.

What did human beings need from this physical world that he was not available in the spirit world? The spirit world lacked the possibility of evolving self-awareness, the possibility of I-being. And this is what humanity lacked. The human self was outside the human being during the most important moments of life, and people lived as in a state of rapture, and in that state they were unaware of being individuals who possessed their own inner life. They were surrendered entirely to the spirit world. They could learn to experience themselves as I-beings only here in the physical world; only here could they attain a real awareness of self. Inseparably connected with self-awareness is what we call the power of reason—modern thinking and perception. Human beings thus had to sacrifice their previous relationship with the spirit world, along with their dim clairvoyance, so that they could acquire the ability to distinguish their I-being from their surroundings, and through this gain self-awareness. In the future, human beings will again acquire this capacity to look clairvoyantly into the world of spirits, while retaining their consciousness of self. The portal of the spirit world has been closed to humankind so that we might become self-aware, inner spiritual beings—so that we could ascend to awareness of self and thus be able to enter the spirit world again as free beings.

Thus, there was a time, long ago, when human beings saw a world entirely different from the one we see today. What meets our eyes when we look at our physical surroundings today? We see a world of minerals, plants, animals, and the physical forms of other human beings. This is the world we find around us: the one to which we belong, the one that is open to us between birth and death. We need the gifts of clairvoyance if we are to penetrate the realm from which our physical world arises, the one behind it. Clairvoyance, as we have said, is not one a normal faculty of human beings today, but in ancient times clairvoyance was available to anyone, given the right conditions. In that clairvoyant state, people came to know the spiritual world. They perceived the spirit beings and spiritual truths that we hear of through spiritual science; they do exist, and one cannot assume they are nonexistent merely because they are invisible to ordinary perception today. Likewise, light and color surround the blind, though not perceptible to them.

At one time, spirit beings were the companions of human beings, who knew, therefore, that they belonged to the spiritual world as beings of spirit and soul. As beings of spirit and soul, they also lived in this world, which told them that the beings they saw around them during clairvoyant states also live in this world. Human beings were companions of beings of spirit and soul during those distant ages of an ancient past.

Even in our time, the knowledge that looks back to those world conditions has always been able to clearly distinguish the various stages through which humankind has passed in different periods of time. First, there was the stage when human beings still lived entirely within the spiritual world—a time when they had barely descended with awareness into the physical, sensory world. Instead, they felt completely connected to the spiritual world, and they drew all their forces from that world of spirit. Spiritual knowledge distinguishes that stage from those that followed, during which spiritual forces gradually disappeared. Instead, a capacity arose that could perceive objects in the phenomenal world in sharp outlines, followed by an elaboration of those impressions through logical thought and discernment. Along with this ability came the definitive I: self-awareness.

Eastern philosophy was able to see into those conditions, because it retained remnants of the ancient, sacred teachings of the Rishis. That philosophy maintained special names for the various periods of human evolution. The most ancient was Krita Yuga, the name given to the clairvoyant periods of human evolution, when clairvoyance ascended into the highest regions of the spiritual world, to beings that we must imagine as the highest of those connected with our world; this was later called the Golden Age.

Another epoch followed, during which human beings saw much less of the spirit world; the effects of the spirit world on human beings had become weaker and less alive. This period was called Treta Yuga and, later, the Silver Age. During this epoch, between birth and death, human beings gained certainty of the spirit world in a different way. Their immediate experiences of the spiritual world were vague, it is true, but to compensate they recalled the time before their birth when they lived with spirit beings. Today, when we grow old, we cannot deny the existence of our youth; similarly, during that period, human beings remained certain of the existence of the spirit world. That age was called Treta Yuga by the wisdom that knows of such things. Later, it was called, less clearly, the Silver Age. These ancient expressions also have deep significance, and it is, in fact, childish for modern science to explain them as it does, since it lacks the vaguest notion about the true origins of those designations.

This Silver Age was followed by an age when there was still clear knowledge of the spiritual world; yet, by that time, human beings had already descended deeply enough into the physical sensory world that they could choose between the two worlds and have beliefs about them. The old clairvoyance grew increasingly dark during the third age, called Dvapara Yuga, or Iron Age. Nevertheless, clairvoyance still existed as a kind of twilight state, and human beings could, because of their belief, connect somewhat with the spirit world. They had previously experienced the spirit world, and they still remembered this during the Iron Age.

Then came the age we designate Kali Yuga, or Dark Age. During this age, the portal of the spiritual world gradually closed completely to human soul faculties. Because human beings had to depend increasingly on their perceptions in the phenomenal world, they were also able to cultivate within this world a feeling of self, or I-being. This age began at a relatively recent date, 3100 B.C., and continued into our era.

We intend to study this now in such a way that we can distinguish these various ages and understand our most important tasks in this present incarnation.

What were people like during Kali Yuga, when Christ descended to the earth? For three thousand years, they had been in an evolutionary stage that limited them to the phenomenal world. It limited people, between birth and death, to taking in only what the physical world offers. If human evolution had continued in this way, human I-being certainly would have continued to grow stronger, but only in an egoistic way. Human beings would have become indulgent and full of desires; they would have enclosed everything coolly within the self. If something else had not occurred, humankind would have lost all awareness of a spiritual world. What occurred at that point?

The real meaning of what happened appears to our souls if we understand that there are definite times of transition in earthly evolution. Many people merely speculate or indulge in abstract philosophy or cultivate some ideology, and they call every age "a time of transition." We must go back as far as the Atlantean time, however, if we want to find the beginning of Krita Yuga. Treta Yuga, on the other hand, still coincided partly with the time of the Holy Rishis, the ancient Indian civilization, but also with the ancient Persian civilization. Dvapara Yuga coincided with later epochs of civilization, with the Egypo-Chaldean times, and a certain dim clairvoyance still existed then. The moment in time when the portals of the spirit world gradually began to close, limiting humanity to the physical plane, began 3,101 years before Jesus Christ walked the earth. Thus we see an age beginning about three thousand years before the Christ event, an age that gradually made us what we are today. Once we realize that it was during that age that the most important event in all of earthly evolution took place— Christ's achievement—we can appreciate its true meaning.

Indeed, we find that almost every period has been called a time of transition—at least, as far back as we can go with the help of the printed word, and so much has been printed. Those who stand on the foundation of spiritual science will not be so free with the use of the word *transition,* because it refers only to those periods in which something takes place that is much more essential and decisive than the events of other ages.

"Nature does not make leaps."[3] This is a statement that official science assumes to be true; anthroposophists, however, should understand that it is meaningless. It sounds objective, but it makes no sense, since nature continually makes leaps. Look at a plant; you find that there is a leap whenever something new appears in its development. There is a leap from leaf formation to the blossom, from the calyx to the petals, from the petals to the stamen, and so on. After nature develops gradually for awhile, it leaps; indeed, all existence makes leaps. This is the essential nature of evolution: crises and leaps. When people say "Nature does not make leaps," it is one of those truisms that arise from the terrible laziness of human thinking. Indeed, nature makes many leaps.

Spiritual life in particular proceeds in leaps. Tremendous and important leaps occur in spiritual development. Life moves forward gradually, until a significant spiritual leap occurs again. A tremendous leap in the life of humanity occurred when Christ walked the earth, one that had importance for more than those who were with him. Thus we can say that the age when Christ lived and taught in Palestine was an age of transition. Please do not believe, however, that such a leap as this must be noticed easily by everyone—certainly not. The most essential events of any age may remain completely hidden from the eyes of those

---

3. See Charles Darwin, *On the Origin of Species by Means of Natural Selection* (1859). Darwin's idea of gradualism states that changes in nature are slow, steady, stately. Given enough time, evolution accounts for all changes in nature.

living at the time, and they may pass by completely unnoticed. We know of such an event, one that left no trace and went unnoticed by millions of people. We know that the important Roman writer Tacitus, in one of his works, described the Christians as a secret and unknown sect. We also know that one hundred years after Christianity had spread over the southern regions of Europe, there were strange tales in Rome about it.

There were thus many groups in Rome at the time that knew nothing of Christianity, except that it was a disturbing sect that existed in some remote backstreet, led by a person named Jesus, who incited people to all kinds of offences. This was one version that was circulated in Rome, even after a century of Christian existence. It demonstrates how the most significant of events—not just for that time but for all of human evolution—occurred without a trace, unnoticed by a vast number of people. We must imagine that, whereas people may notice absolutely nothing, the most important and meaningful event may be taking place. Although people may say that we live in a time when nothing essential or important is happening, it does not mean they are right.

It is a fact that we are now living again in an age of transition, one in which the most important spiritual events are taking place. They are largely unknown to our contemporaries, yet they are nevertheless happening. We need to be very clear about this: we can talk about periods of transition, but we should not use such words too freely. What was the essential characteristic of that age of transition during which Jesus Christ appeared? It is expressed in those significant words that we must understand in the right way. It was the prophecy of John the Baptist, expressed later by Christ: Change the disposition of your souls; the kingdoms of heaven are at hand. This saying contains a whole world, and it is precisely this world that is so intimately connected with the most important of events, consummated then for human evolution as a whole.[4]

Through natural evolution during Kali Yuga, human beings gradually attained power of discernment and I-awareness, but they lost the ability to connect with the spirit world through their own powers. John the Baptist was saying that the time had come to train self-awareness so that the I could completely penetrate the depths of one's soul to find its inner connection with the kingdoms of heaven. In other words, ordinary human beings could no longer ascend clairvoyantly outside themselves into a spirit world. Instead, the kingdoms of heaven had to descend to the physical world and reveal themselves in such a way that the I could recognize spiritual reality through the sense for truth inherent in ordinary self-awareness. People had to change the previous disposition of their souls, so that they could be confident that soul life could be warmed within the I, and one could be certain of a spiritual world by observing surrounding phenomena. Human beings had to learn to comprehend the spiritual worlds through I-consciousness. Spiritual worlds had descended and were near, and they must no longer be sought in a world of rapture, outside consciousness.

Consequently, the Christ had to descend and appear in a physical human body, because the disposition of the human soul was attuned to comprehending physical phenomena. God had to come to human beings on the physical plane, because I-being had developed and the portal to the spiritual world had

---

4. The King James version: In those days came John the Baptist, preaching in the wilderness of Judaea, and saying, Repent ye: for the kingdom of heaven is at hand" (Matt. 3:1–2); "Jesus began to preach, and to say, Repent: for the kingdom of heaven is at hand" (Matt. 4:17).

closed; humankind could no longer approach the gods in the old way. Here we see the greatness of the event at that time: through the natural evolution of human faculties, the old relationship with the spiritual worlds was lost, replaced by I-consciousness. But it was also possible, as a result, to become conscious of these spirit worlds within the physical world. Christ thus became the mediator of the spirit worlds for those who have reached the stage of development where they can connect with the spiritual world in the I, which lives on the physical plane. "Change the disposition of your souls"—in other words, do not believe that ordinary human beings can now ascend to the spirit world through rapture; rather, through the development of capacities inherent in I-being and with the help of Christ, you can find the path leading to spirit worlds. This is the only way that humanity can find the spirit now.

Today we are living in a similar age. Since Kali Yuga, the Dark Age, ended in 1899, new soul faculties are once again being slowly prepared in a similar way. It is very possible that our contemporaries, those living in our age, may sleep through this. Gradually, we will learn to recognize what needs to take place for all humanity during the age that began at the end of Kali Yuga. It is our task to see that this transitional event does not pass by unnoticed and without affecting human progress.

Kali Yuga ended only a few years ago, around 1899. We are now approaching a time when, in addition to evolved self-awareness, certain clairvoyant faculties will be regained naturally. Human beings will have the strange and remarkable experience of not knowing what is really happening to them. People will begin to receive premonitions that become reality; they will be able to foresee events that actually occur. Indeed, people everywhere will gradually begin to see what we call the human ether body, though only as a vague outline and in its first elements. Human beings today see only the physical body; the capacity to see the ether body will gradually be added. People will either learn that this ether body is real, or believe that it is a sensory illusion, since such a thing, so they will say, does not exist. Things will reach the point where many people who have these experiences will wonder if they are insane

Although only a small number of people will develop these faculties during the next few decades, spiritual science will spread, because we feel a responsibility toward something that is really happening; it must take place according to the natural course of events. Why do we teach spiritual science? Because phenomena will appear in the near future that only spiritual science will be able to understand; it will be misunderstood without spiritual science.

In a few people, these faculties will develop relatively quickly. It is true, certainly, that even today people can ascend, through esoteric training, far beyond what is beginning on a small scale for humanity. At the same time, the goal to which we can ascend today through the appropriate self-development is already being prepared somewhat for all of humanity. It will be necessary to speak of this, whether people understand it or not, between 1930 and 1940. Only a few decades separate us from the time when such phenomena will be more frequent.

By that time, however, something else will occur for those who will have acquired these faculties. They will receive proof of one of the most powerful sayings in the New Testament, which will deeply move their souls. These words will arise in their souls: "Lo, I am with you always, even unto the end of the world" (Matt. 28:20), that is (if translated correctly), "even to the end of the eons of earth." This expression tells us that

Christianity is not merely as described in books or as learned in recent times. They tell us that Christianity is more than some dogma to be embraced; it is alive and contains the vision and experience of revelations, something that will continue to unfold with increasing strength. We are only at the beginning of the activity of Christianity, and those who have truly united with Christ know that new revelations will continually spring from it. They know that Christianity is not diminishing but growing and becoming; it is living, not dead.

One who takes up spiritual development today can already begin to experience the truth of "Lo, I am with you always, even unto the end of the eons of the earth." The Christ is with us and hovers over the earth in spirit. Before the event of Golgotha, clairvoyants were unable to find Christ in the earth's atmosphere. Christ was not visible in the earth's atmosphere until after the event of Golgotha, because he was not there. Those who were experienced in clairvoyance before Christian times knew that the time would come when this would happen. They knew that it was not yet possible to find what one calls the Christ within the astral sphere of our earth. They knew that the time would come when the clairvoyant eye opens to see Christ in the earthly sphere. They knew that a great change would take place in earthly clairvoyance, and yet they were not advanced enough so that the events in Palestine would convince them that this had already taken place. No physical events could convince them that Christ had already descended to earth.

Only one thing could convince them: they had to see the Christ clairvoyantly in the atmosphere of the earth. Thus they were convinced that Christ's descent to earth—as predicted by the mysteries—had in fact been consummated. People today can train themselves to experience clairvoyantly what Paul experienced as the presence of Christ in the atmosphere of the earth. This is also what a few individuals here and there will be able to experience through a natural clairvoyance (as I have already described it), from 1930 to 1940. This will continue through long periods of time and become entirely natural to humankind.

The event of Damascus will repeat itself for many people, and we can call this event a return of Christ in the spirit. Christ will be present for all those who will be able to ascend far enough to see the ether body. Christ descended only once in the flesh, when he lived in Palestine, but he is always present in his ether body within the etheric atmosphere of the earth. Because human beings will be able to develop etheric vision, they will also be able to see him. The return of Christ will thus come to pass for humanity, because people will advance to the faculty of seeing Christ in the ether. This is what we may look forward to in our time of transition. It is the task of spiritual science to prepare human souls to receive Christ, who has come down to them.

We see that we have already considered the second question we posed. We have seen that it makes good sense to use our incarnations well, and we have also seen that the best use is to prepare ourselves for understanding the future of Christ. We must learn to understand this return of Christ in the right way. We will then be able to understand the great dangers connected with it. I must now explain this to you. The most sublime human experience possible is now waiting for humankind in what I described as the return of Christ in the spirit. Yet modern materialism will continue to exert such strength that even this fact will be misinterpreted in a materialistic way, and that interpretation will become reality. This fact will be interpreted as a return of Christ in the flesh, and false christs and messiahs will walk the earth in the near future—people who claim to be the Christ returned. Anthroposophists, however, should be not be deceived by materialists who believe that Christ can descend again to earth in the flesh. They know that Kali Yuga has ended—the age in which human beings, for the development of I-being, needed life within physical matter and without the ability to see into the spirit worlds. People must now develop themselves to rise into the spiritual sphere, where they can see the Christ alive and always present in the ether realm.

Humanity will be given approximately 2,500 years to develop these faculties. This time will be at our disposal to develop etheric vision as a natural, universal human faculty, after which humankind will advance to another faculty in another time of transition. During these 2,500 years, human souls will increasingly develop these faculties in themselves. It will make no difference whether they are living between birth and death or in the spirit world after death. Human life between death and rebirth will also pass differently for those who have experienced the reappearance of Christ; life after death will change as a result of this experience. This is why it is so important for the souls now incarnated to prepare for the Christ event during this century. This is equally important for those who will be physically incarnated on earth and for those who have passed through the portal of death and will be living the life between death and a new birth. It is extremely important for every soul alive today to prepare for this event and, thereby, become well armed against the dangers.

When we speak in this way, we get a sense of what anthroposophy should and can mean to us and how it should prepare us to fulfill our task by assuring that such a sublime event does not pass humanity by without a trace. If it were to pass unnoticed, humanity would forfeit its most important possibility for evolution, thus sinking into darkness and eventual death. This event can bring light to human beings only if they awaken to this new perception and open up to the new Christ event.

This will be repeated again and again in the near future; at the same time, it must be said repeatedly that the false prophets could prevent the good and the great if they were they to succeed in spreading the notion that Christ will appear again in the flesh. If anthroposophists fail to understand this, they may fall prey to an illusion that would enable false messiahs to arise. False messiahs will appear; they will depend on souls who are so weakened by materialism that they cannot imagine anything else as Christ's reappearance—only that he must appear in the flesh. This misinterpretation of prophecy is evil, and it will appear as a dangerous temptation for humanity. It is the task of anthroposophy to protect humankind from this temptation. This cannot be emphasized too strongly for all who have ears to hear. We can see, moreover, that anthroposophy has important messages. We do not "pursue" anthroposophy merely because we are curious about various facts, but because we know that these facts must be used to save and eventually perfect humanity.

The Christ will appear later to humanity in many forms. The form he chose for the events in Palestine was chosen because, at that time, human beings needed to develop their consciousness on the physical plane and, through this, conquer the physical world. Humanity is called on to develop increasingly higher faculties, so that the course of evolution can, again and again, make new leaps.

Christ will be there so that human beings can experience him through those higher stages of knowledge. Christianity, in this sense, is not at the end but at the beginning of its influence. Humanity will continue to advance from stage to stage, and Christianity will be there at every stage to satisfy the deepest needs of the human soul throughout all the future ages of earth.

3 · Buddhism and Pauline Christianity

Köln, February 27, 1910

Today, based on research that can be done in higher worlds, we will see how significant it is to experience what the future holds in store for humanity. The mission of the spiritual scientific movement is related to the important events of this transitional period in which we live. From this, we can be certain that much still lies before us in the future, and thus we look to spiritual science for guidance in taking the appropriate action in the present. We must understand, then, the special significance of cognition, feeling, and volition in our time.

There is a tremendous distinction between the spiritual stream that came from Buddha and the one that arose from the Christ impulse. This is not meant to place these streams in opposition to each other; rather, we need to understand how each of these streams can be fruitful. They must unite in the future, and Christianity must be fructified by spiritual science. Christianity had to set aside the teaching of reincarnation for awhile. It was included in the esoteric teaching, but could not be received in exoteric Christianity for certain universal pedagogical reasons. In contrast, reincarnation has been a fundamental principle of Buddhism, where it is connected with the teaching of suffering, and this is exactly what Christianity is intended to overcome. Once we recognize the purposes and missions of each stream, we can also distinguish clearly between them. The main distinction can be seen most clearly when we examine two individuals: Buddha and Paul.

Gautama Buddha came to knowledge through enlightenment under the Bodhi tree. He then taught that this world is maya. It cannot be considered real, because within it is maya, the great illusion that one takes as reality. Human beings must strive for release from the realm of the elements, after which they enter the realm of Nirvana, where neither names nor things exist. Only then is one freed from illusion. The realm of maya is suffering: birth, disease, old age, and death. It is the thirst for existence that brings human beings into this realm. Once people have been freed of this thirst, they no longer need to incarnate. We may ask why the great Buddha preached this doctrine, and, to find the answer, we must take a look at human evolution.

Human beings were not always as they are today. In earlier times, people not only had physical bodies at their disposal to achieve knowledge, but, diffused among human beings, there was also a kind of clairvoyant knowledge. They knew that there were spiritual hierarchies, just as we know that there are plants. They were lacking in the power of discernment, but they could see the creative beings. This wisdom gradually disappeared, but a memory of it remained. In ancient India and Persia, and even in Egypt, there was still a memory of previous earthly lives. The human soul was such that people knew that they had descended from divine beings, but they also knew that their incarnations gradually sank into the physical to the degree that their spiritual sight had been darkened.

Human beings experienced progress then as degeneration and a step backward. This was felt, even in much later times, especially by those who were still able to leave their physical bodies. To them, the everyday world appeared in those moments to be illusory and deceptive. Buddha spoke only of what lived in the human soul. The physical, sensory world was experienced as one that pulled humankind down; they wanted to leave this world and ascend. They blamed the world of the senses for the descent of humanity.

Let us compare this concept with the Christ impulse and the teachings of Paul. He did not call the sensory world an illusion, though he knew as well as Buddha that humankind had descended from the spiritual worlds and that it was the human urge for existence that brings us into this world. Speaking in a Christian sense, however, let us ask if this urge for existence is necessarily bad. Is the physical, sensory world simply a deception? According to Paul's view, it is not the urge for existence that is evil. Originally, this urge was good, but it became harmful through the fall of humankind, under the influence of luciferic beings. Although this urge was not always harmful, it has become detrimental, bringing sickness, lies, suffering, and so on. In the Buddha's view, this is a cosmic event; in Paul's view, it is a human event.

If luciferic influences had not interfered, humanity would have seen the truth of the physical world instead of illusion. It is not the sensory world that is wrong, but human knowledge dulled by luciferic influences. The difference in these views offer different answers. Buddha looked for redemption in a world where nothing of the sensory world remained. Paul said that people should purify their forces, the thirst for existence, because it was people themselves who had corrupted them.

Human beings should tear the veil from the truth and, through purification, regain sight of the truth they had covered. In place of the veil that conceals the plant world, for example, we will see divine spiritual forces at work behind the plants. Rend the veil, and the world of the senses becomes transparent; we finally see the realm of spirit. We believed we saw the animal, plant, and mineral kingdoms, and that was our error. In truth, it was the hierarchies flowing toward us.

That is why Paul taught not to kill the pleasure of existence but to purify it, because it was originally good.[1] This can happen when people receive the power of Christ. When this power permeates the soul, it drives away the soul's darkness. The gods did not place humankind on the earth without purpose; it is our duty to overcome what prevents us from seeing this world in spirit. The Buddha's conclusion—that we must avoid incarnation—points to an archetypal wisdom for humanity. Paul, by contrast, taught that we should go through incarnation, imbuing ourselves with Christ, and that, in the distant future, all the illusions of humanity will vanish.[2] This teaching blames people themselves rather than the sensory world, and it had to become a historic doctrine. It is exactly for this reason, however, that it could not be given fully to begin with. Only the initial impulse could be given, which must be penetrated. This impulse would then gradually enter every area of life. Almost two thousand years have passed since the Mystery of Golgotha, but today the

---

1. "For the kingdom of God is not meat and drink; but righteousness, and peace, and joy in the Holy Ghost" (Rom. 14:17).

2. "But when that which is perfect is come, then that which is in part shall be done away. When I was a child, I spake as a child, I understood as a child, I thought as a child: but when I became a man, I put away childish things. For now we see through a glass, darkly; but then face to face: now I know in part; but then shall I know even as also I am known" (I Cor. 13:10–12).

Christ impulse is only beginning to be received. Whole areas of life, such as philosophy and science, have yet to be imbued with it. The Buddha was better able to give his teaching all at once, because he referred to an ancient wisdom that was still experienced in his time. The Christ impulse, however, must prevail gradually. An epistemology based on these facts contrasts sharply with that of Kant, who failed to realize that it is our knowledge itself that must be purified.

Paul had to tell people that the work of each individual incarnation is indeed very important. In contrast to the relatively recent doctrine of the Buddha—that the individual incarnation is worthless—he almost had to overstate this teaching. One must learn to say, "Not I, but Christ in me." This is the purified I. Through Paul, the spiritual life came to depend on this one incarnation for all the future. Now that this soul education has been completed and enough human beings have gone through it in the last two thousand years, it is time again to teach reincarnation and karma. We must try to restore I-being to its condition before it began to incarnate.

It is always said that Christ is constantly with us. "I am with you every day until the end of the earth" (Matt. 28:20). Now, we must learn to see Christ and know that what we see is real. This will happen soon, even in this century, and increasingly during the next two thousand years. How will this happen? Look at the way people view our planet today. Science describes it mechanically, chemically, and physically or uses ideas such as the Kant-Laplace theory.[3] Nevertheless, we are approaching a reversal in these areas. A view will arise and see

---

3. Immanuel Kant (1724–1804) proposed a theory of how the solar system was formed, and his theory was elaborated by the French mathematician and astronomer Simon LaPlace (1749–1827).

the earth in terms of plant, or what could be called ether forces, not in terms of purely mineral forces. The plant directs its root toward the earth's center, and its upper part stands in relation to the sun. These are the forces that form the earth; gravity is secondary.

Plants preceded minerals, just as coal was once plant life; this will soon be discovered. Plants give the planet its form and produce the substance that leads to its mineral foundation. The beginning of this idea was given through Goethe in his plant morphology, which was not understood. One will gradually begin to see the etheric world, because it is characteristic of the plant realm. Once people are able to receive the growth forces of the plant kingdom, they will be released from the forces that now prevent human beings from seeing the Christ. Spiritual science should help, but this will not be possible as long as people believe that the ascent of the physical into the etheric has nothing to do with the inner human being. In a laboratory, it is not important whether one's moral character is strong or weak, but this is not the case when we are concerned with ether forces; here our moral constitution affects the results. Consequently, it is impossible for people today to develop this ability unless they change. The laboratory table must become an altar, just as it was for Goethe, who, as a child, illuminated his small altar to nature with the rising sun.

This will happen before long. Those who can say "Not I, but Christ in me," will be able to work with plant forces, just as we now work with mineral forces.[4] Our inner being and our outer environment interact reciprocally; what is outside transforms

---

4. "I am crucified with Christ: nevertheless I live; yet not I, but Christ liveth in me: and the life which I now live in the flesh I live by the faith of the Son of God, who loved me, and gave himself for me" (Gal. 2:20).

itself for us, depending on whether our vision is clear or clouded. Even in this century, and increasingly throughout the next 2,500 years, people will begin to see Christ in an etheric form. They will see the etheric earth, from which the plant world emerges. They will also be able to see that inner goodness affects the environment in a different way than does evil.

The one who possesses this science in the highest degree is the Maitreya Buddha, who will come approximately three thousand years from now. The name *Maitreya Buddha* means the "Buddha of right mindedness."[5] He is the one who will make human beings aware of the significance of right thinking. This will lead humankind to an understanding of the proper direction for the future. You must transform abstract ideals into concrete ideals before you can contribute to evolution in a way that moves it forward. If we do not succeed in this, the earth will sink into materialism, and humanity will have to begin again, either on the earth after a great catastrophe, or on the next planet.[6] The earth needs anthroposophy. Those who realize this are anthroposophists.

---

5. *Maitreya* (Sanskrit), literally, "filled with loving kindness."
6. The next planetary stage is Jupiter; see Rudolf Steiner, *An Outline of Esoteric Science* (Anthroposophic Press, 1999), chapter 4; and *The Apocalypse of St. John* (Anthroposophic Press, 1993), lecture 9.

4 • Mysteries of the Universe: Comets and the Moon

Stuttgart, March 5, 1910

At night, when the stars are clear and we look into the expanse of the heavens, a feeling of exaltation flows through our souls as we let the infinite wonders of the stars affect us. The intensity of this feeling varies from person to person, according to character. When faced with the starry heavens, however, one soon becomes aware of a longing to understand these cosmic wonders. And one is not the least deterred by the thought that this feeling of exaltation and grandeur might vanish because of the desire to comprehend the mystery of the starry world; it is reasonable to believe that this feeling will not be harmed by understanding and comprehension. As with anything, it becomes more or less obvious that spiritual scientific knowledge enhances and strengthens our feelings and experiences, as long as we have a healthy, practical understanding. Similarly, we become confident that the sublime nature of our feelings toward cosmic realities will not diminish with our understanding of what passes through space or appears fixed.

As in any presentation, of course, we can address only a small corner of the world, so we must take time to understand the facts of the world step by step. Today we will be concerned with a small, trifling part of space as it relates to human life. Although we may sense this in a vague way, through spiritual science we get a more exact understanding of how we are born out of the totality of the universe and how cosmic mysteries relate to uniquely human mysteries. This becomes especially clear when we investigate certain mysteries of existence with precision.

A polarity manifests in human life as it evolves on earth—a polarity that is found everywhere and always: the contrast between masculine and feminine. We know that this polarity in humankind has existed since ancient Lemuria, and we know, too, that it will last for a certain period in our earthly existence and ultimately resolve again into a higher unity.[1]

Recall that all human life comes from cosmic life, and then ask: If the polarity between man and woman has existed in human life and, to a certain extent, accompanied earthly evolution since ancient Lemurian times, is there something in the cosmos that represents this polarity at a higher level? Can we find something in the cosmos that manifests on earth as masculine and feminine?

This question can be answered, but if we stand on the foundation of spiritual science, we cannot proceed according to the principles of modern materialists. Materialists cannot visualize anything but the phenomena of their immediate environment, and they are thus prone to look for this male-female polarity in everything, whereas it now applies only to human and animal life on earth. This is an offense of our time. We must bear clearly in mind that, strictly speaking, we can apply the terms

---

1. See Rudolf Steiner, *Cosmic Memory: Prehistory of Earth and Man* (Garber, 1990; GA 11), chapters 5 and 6.

masculine and *feminine* to humankind only as it has existed since the Lemurian epoch and up to a certain point in earthly evolution, and insofar as animals and plants are concerned, only during ancient Moon and earth evolution. This question, however, still remains: Did male and female, as they exist on earth, arise from a higher, cosmic polarity? If were to discover this polarity, we would see a wonderful and mysterious relationship between this and a certain cosmic phenomenon. Polarity exists everywhere in the cosmos, of course, but we must understand how to look for it in the right way.

The first cosmic polarity that is significant for human life is that between sun and earth. In our various studies of earthly evolution, we have seen how the sun separated from our earth and how they became independent bodies in space. We may ask, however: How is the contrast between sun and earth in the macrocosm represented in a human being, the microcosm? Is there a contrast in the human being that corresponds to the contrast between sun and earth in our planetary system? Yes, there is. It occurs in the human organism (both physical and spiritual) between the outer expression of the head's structure and the outer expression of the human organs of movement, the hands and feet. Everything expressed in this contrast between the head and the organs of movement in a human being corresponds to the cosmic polarity between sun and earth. We shall soon see how this is also consistent with the relationship between the sun and the human heart. The point is, however, that in the human being there is the head on the one hand, and what we call the organs of movement on the other.

You can readily understand that, insofar as the limbs were concerned, human beings were completely different during the ancient Moon evolution. It was earth that moved humankind into an upright position so that we can use our hands and feet as we do today. Again, it was only on the earth that the human head was enabled to look freely into cosmic space, because the sun's forces lifted the human being into an upright position, whereas the spine had been horizontal during the ancient Moon evolution. We may say that earth is responsible for our ability to use our legs and feet as we do today. The sun affected the earth from outside and formed a polarity with the earth; thus the human head freed itself, in a sense, from bondage to the earth, resulting in our ability to look freely into space.

The polarity in the planetary system between sun and earth appears in the human being as the polarity between head and limbs. We find this polarity in every human being, whether man or woman, and in this sense, men and women are essentially alike. Therefore, we can say that this polarity between sun and earth is expressed the same way in both men and women. The earth affects men and women to the same degree; women are bound to the earth in the same way men are; the sun frees the head—whether that of a man or a woman—from bondage to the earth.

We can gauge the depth of this polarity if we recall that those beings who fell into dense matter too early (mammals) were unable to gain free sight into cosmic space; their appearance is bound to earthly existence. For the mammals, the contrast between sun and earth did not become a contrast in their own being in the same way. Consequently, we cannot speak of mammals as microcosms as we can human beings; we see the microcosmic nature of humankind in the contrast between head and limbs.

This example shows the infinite importance of not becoming unbalanced our studies. We can count the bones of a human being and the bones of higher mammals, and we can count the muscles of a human being and those of mammals; the conclusion one can draw from this has led to a modern worldview that places humankind close to the higher mammals. This can happen because people have not yet learned through spiritual science that it is not good enough just to *have* the facts; we must add something to them.

Be aware that something very important is being said here— something that anthroposophists need to inscribe in their hearts and remember. Many things are true, but it is not enough merely to know that something is true. For example, modern natural science claims a kinship between humankind and apes, and it is undoubtedly true. The important thing, however, is not merely to possess a fact, but to recognize its importance for explaining existence as a whole. Simply because its importance is not recognized, one may fail to see the decisive nature of a seemingly common, everyday fact.

There is one truth, familiar to everyone, that becomes deeply significant for our whole doctrine of earthly evolution, once its true importance is understood: the fact that humankind is the only earthly being who can look freely into cosmic space. If we compare human beings in this sense with apes, who are closely related, we must say that, although apes have tried to raise themselves into an upright stance, somehow they made a mess of it; this is the point. We must understand the relative value of a fact. We must *feel* the importance of the fact that human beings have this advantage, and then we can also relate it to the cosmic fact just described: that it is not just the earth, but the sun in contrast to the earth—something beyond earth—that renders human beings citizens of heavenly space and tears us from earthly existence. In a sense, we can say that this whole cosmic adjustment, which we now recognize as the polarity between sun and earth, had to occur so that human beings could take their place of honor in our universe. This constellation of sun and earth had to be brought about for the sake of humankind, that we might be raised from an animal posture. We have the same polarity in human beings, therefore, that we see sun an its counterpart the earth.

Now the question arises: Can we see in the cosmos another contrast found on earth: the male-female polarity? Might there be something in our solar system that brings about the contrast between man and woman as a kind of mirror image on earth? Certainly; this higher polarity can be seen in the polarity between comets and the moon. Just as our head and limbs reflect the sun-earth polarity, male and female reflect the comet-moon polarity.

This leads us into deep cosmic mysteries. Though it may sound strange, it is a fact that, in various degrees, the members of the physical human body express the spirit behind them. In the human physical body, the head (and, in a different sense, the limbs) correspond in appearance most closely to the underlying, inner, spiritual forces. Let us be clear about this: everything we face in the physical world is an image of spirit, since spirit formed it. When spirit forms something physical, it can form it in such a way that, at a certain stage of evolution, that physical form either resembles it or looks quite different. Only the human head and limbs resemble their spiritual counterparts in terms of external structure. The rest of the human body does not resemble the spiritual image at all. The outer human structure (except the head and limbs) is a mirage in the most profound sense, and those with developed clairvoyance always see human beings in such a way that only the head and limbs make a real impression. Head and limbs give a clairvoyant the sense that they are true and do not deceive. The rest of the human body, however, gives clairvoyant consciousness the feeling that it is false in form—something that has deteriorated and does not at all resemble the spirit behind it. Moreover, everything that is feminine appears to clairvoyant consciousness as though it did not advance beyond a certain stage of evolution, but remained behind.

We can say that evolution has advanced from point *A* to *B*. If *C* represented normal development, we would be at point *C* in terms of the

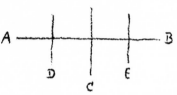

human head and limbs. What appears as the form of a female body has remained as though it were still at *D* and not developing. Do not misunderstand when we say that the female body, as it is today, remained behind at a more spiritual stage; its form has not descended as deeply enough into matter to be in accord with the general stage of evolution. Except for the head and limbs, however, the male body has gone beyond this general stage. It went beyond this stage and reached point *E*. Thus the male body has deteriorated and become more physical than its spiritual archetype, since it descended more deeply into the material than it needed to for the general stage of evolution. There is something in the female body, therefore, that remained behind normal evolution, and in the male body there is something that descended more deeply into the physical than did the head and limbs.

This same polarity is also found in our solar system. If we look at our earth and the sun as normal evolutionary stages, we see that the comet has not advanced to the normal stage. In our cosmos, it corresponds to the feminine in humankind. Thus we must view cometary existence as the cosmic archetype of the female organization. Lunar existence is the counterpart of male existence. This will be clear from what was said before; we know that the moon is a piece of the earth that had to separate. If it had remained a part of earth, the earth could not have moved forward in its evolution. The moon had to be separated because of its density. In the cosmos, the polarity between comet and moon is thus the archetype of the human polarity of female and male.

This is very interesting, because it shows us that, whether we consider an earthly being such as humankind or the whole universe, we must not merely think of one aspect with others as they appear spatially; to do this is to give in to a terrible illusion. The various members of a human organism are, of course, adjacent to one another, and the ordinary materialistic anatomist will consider them to be at the same stage of development. Those who study the truth of things, however, see the differences, inasmuch as one member has reached a certain point of evolution, another has not (though it has progressed somewhat), and yet another has gone beyond that point. A time will come when the whole human organism will be studied in this way; only then will there be a true esoteric study of anatomy. As I said, things that are adjacent may nevertheless exist at different stages of evolution, and human bodily organs can be understood only when you realize that each has reached a different stage of evolution.

If you recall that the ancient Moon preceded our earth evolution, what we have said will show you that, although the present moon is certainly one aspect of the ancient Moon, it has moved on and no longer represents that stage. The moon has not only advanced to the stage of earth but has gone beyond it. The moon could not wait until the earth reached the Jupiter stage, and therefore it has became sluggish in its physical aspect, though not in its spiritual relationships, of course.

Comets represent the relationship between the ancient Moon and the sun that prevailed at a certain time during the ancient Moon evolution. Comets remain at that stage, but now they must express this in a somewhat different way. Comets have not advanced to the general point of earthly existence. The present moon represents part of the later Jupiter stage; it was born far too early and has thus slowed down and become incapable of life. Similarly, comets contain a portion of the ancient Moon existence, which projects into our present earthly evolution.

Parenthetically, I would like to add an important point, through which our spiritual scientific ways of studying have won a little triumph. In 1906, I gave eighteen lectures in Paris on cosmogony.[2] Those who were there may recall that I spoke of certain matters not mentioned in my *Outline of Esoteric Science*. One cannot present everything at once; it takes endless books to develop everything. In Paris, I developed a point having to do with the physical and chemical aspect of the subject, as it were. I spoke of the ancient Moon evolution and how it projects into present cometary existence, because comets have remained at that earlier stage and, to the extent current conditions allow, expresses those old relationships in its laws. This ancient Moon evolution differs from that of earth, since nitrogen and certain nitrous compounds (cyanide and prussic acid)

---

2. *An Esoteric Cosmology*, 18 lectures in Paris, May 25–June 14, 1906 (Garber, 1987; GA 94).

were just as necessary to the beings on the ancient Moon as oxygen is to the beings of our earth. Cyanide and similar compounds are deadly to the life of higher beings and lead to their destruction. Yet compounds of carbon and nitrogen, prussic acid, and the like, played a similar role there to that of oxygen on earth.

These matters were developed in Paris from the whole scope of spiritual science. Those who recall these facts would have to say that, if this is true, there must be proof that something like compounds of carbon and nitrogen exist in comets today. You may recall that the newspapers are now saying that the existence of cyanide compounds has been proved in the spectrum of the comet (this information was brought to my attention during lectures on St. John and the other three Gospels in Stockholm[3]). This is a brilliant confirmation of what spiritual research was able to say earlier, and it has finally been confirmed by physical science. Proofs of this sort are always being asked of us, so it is quoted here. When such a striking case is available, it is important for anthroposophists to point it out and—without pride—to remind ourselves of a small triumph for spiritual science.

So you see, we can truly say that the polarity between masculine and feminine has a cosmic archetype in the polarity between comet and moon. Naturally, it is impossible to go into all the ramifications, but if we could proceed from this and show the full effect of the moon and comets, you would realize the great power it is for the soul, surpassing all general feelings of sublimity. You would get a sense of how we see this polarity

---

3. These eleven lectures (January 2–15, 1910) on the Gospels and the European mysteries took place in Sweden. They have not been published in English.

reflected here on earth, and how its function expresses exactly the polarity between comet and moon in the universe. It is possible to indicate only a few of these matters. But some are very important, and we will touch on them.

Above all, we must become conscious of how the polarity between comet and moon affects human beings. We must not think that this contrast is expressed only through the man and woman in humanity; we must be clear that masculine characteristics exist in every woman, and feminine characteristics in every man. We also know that the ether body of a man is female, and that the ether body of a woman is male; this immediately makes the matter extremely complicated. We must realize that the male-female polarity is thus reversed in the ether bodies of men and women, as are the cometary and lunar effects. These effects are also present in relation to the astral body and I-being. Hence, the contrast between comet and moon has a deep, incisive significance for human evolution on earth. The fact that Moon evolution is mysteriously connected with the relationship between the sexes (a connection that eludes exoteric thinking) can be seen in something that might seem entirely accidental: that the product of a union between male and female, a child, needs ten lunar months to develop, from conception to birth. Even modern science does not deal with solar months, but with lunar months. This is because, there, the relationship between the moon (representing the universal masculine) and the cometary nature (representing the universal feminine) is decisive and reflects itself in the product of the sexes.

Feminine spiritual life, whether in a man or in a woman, projects something primitive and elemental into our existence, and this is also what a comet does. Wherever this male-female polarity confronts us, we see it because it is expressed with unusual clarity. If we look at this from the other side—the comets—we have another important consequence for human evolution. Cometary nature is feminine, so to speak, and in the movements and occasional appearance of comets, we have a kind of archetypal projection of feminine nature in the cosmos. It gives the impression of having come to a halt before reaching the normal, general stage of evolution. This cosmic feminine (the expression is not quite right, but we lack suitable terms) occasionally shoots in and stirs our existence from the depths of pre-history, so to speak. In the mode of its appearance, a comet resembles the feminine. We can also express it this way: a woman acts more out of passion and feeling, in contrast to dry, masculine reasoning; similarly, it is the regular, reasonable course of the moon related to the cometary phenomenon that projects into our existence in a seemingly irregular way. This is the unique nature of feminine spiritual life. Please note, however, that I do not mean the spiritual life of woman per se, but feminine spiritual life. There is a difference. The spiritual life of a woman naturally includes masculine characteristics.

Those who judge everything by appearances criticize spiritual science because of the number of women who are drawn to it today. They do not realize that this is understandable, simply because the average brain of a man has overstepped a certain general point of evolution; it has become drier, more wooden, and thus clings more rigidly to traditional concepts. It cannot free itself from the prejudices in which it is stuck. Men who study spiritual science may occasionally find it difficult in this incarnation to utilize this masculine brain. The male brain is stiff, resistant, and more difficult to manipulate than a female brain, which easily overcomes obstacles that a male brain erects through its density. Consequently, the female brain can more quickly follow what is new in our view of the world. To the extent that the male and female principles are expressed in the structure of the human brain, it may even be said that, in our time, it is very uncomfortable and unpleasant to be forced to use a male brain, which must be trained much more carefully, much more radically, than a female brain. So you can see that it is not really extraordinary that women today find their bearings more easily in something as new as spiritual science.

These facts are very important in terms of cultural history, but just about the only place we can discuss them today is in anthroposophic groups. Except for our groups, who will seriously consider the fact that a male brain is less comfortable than a female brain? Naturally, despite these facts, there are many female brains that bear thoroughly masculine traits. These things are more complicated than assumed by modern notions.

Cometary nature is elemental; it stirs things up and, in a sense, is needed so that evolution is supported properly by the cosmos. People have always suspected that cometary nature is connected in some way with earthly existence. It is only in our day that such an idea is rejected. Just imagine the look on the face of today's typical scholar if confronted by the conversation between Professor Bode and Hegel.[4] Speaking to an orthodox German professor, Hegel flatly stated that good wine years follow the appearance of comets. He supported his argument by pointing to 1811 and 1819, good wine years that were preceded by cometary events. This stirred things up considerably.

---

4. Johann Elert Bode (1747–1826), German astronomer who formulated the relative distances of planets from the sun. Georg Wilhelm Friedrich Hegel (1770–1831), a German philosopher who strongly influenced Karl Marx.

Hegel said that his statement was no less sound than many calculations concerning the courses of stars—that it was an empirical matter, verified by these two cases. Even apart from such humorous episodes, however, people have always presumed ideas such as this one.

We cannot go into details now, which is an endless task, but it would be useful to illuminate one important influence in human evolution. Comets appear at great intervals of time. Let us ask: When comets appear, do they affect overall human evolution by, as it were, stirring up the feminine principle in human nature? Halley's Comet, for example, has a particular reality.[5] This can also be said of many other comets. Halley's Comet has a particular task, and everything it brings has a certain connection to that task. Halley's Comet (we are speaking of its spiritual nature) has the task of impressing its own particular essence on human nature, so that this essence and human nature take a step in the development of the human I whenever the comet approaches the earth. This step leads the I outward to physical concepts. First, the comet has a special influence on the two lower members of human nature: its male and female natures. There it joins the activity of the moon. When a comet is not present, the moon's activity is imbalanced, but the presence of a comet influences the moon's effects.

This is how the effects of the comet are expressed today: whenever the human I takes a step forward, the physical and ether bodies must be transformed in a corresponding way so that the *whole* human being evolves. So that the I can think differently in the nineteenth century from the way it did in the

5. Named for Edmond Halley (1656–1742), from 239 B.C. until 1986, the orbit of Halley's Comet varied from 76 years (1986) and 79.3 years (451 and 1066). It is expected again around 2061.

eighteenth century, something must change the outer expression of the I in the physical and ether bodies; that "something" is the comet. Comets work on the human physical and ether bodies in such a way that they actually create organs—delicate organs suited to further development of human I-being, especially as it has developed since the Christ impulse was integrated with the earth. Since then, cometary appearances mean that the human I, as it develops from stage to stage, gains an increasing use of the physical and etheric organs.

Just think of it; as strange as it may sound—and as crazy as our contemporaries find it—it is true that, during the 1850s, the thinking of materialists such as Büchner or Moleschott would not have been as materialistic if they had not possessed the right physical and etheric brains.[6] The worthy Büchner might otherwise have made a good, average clergyman. For him to arrive at the conclusions in *Kraft und Stoff*, it was not only necessary for his I to have evolved in this way, but also for a corresponding arrangement to be present in the physical and ether bodies. If wish to know the evolutionary state of I-being itself, we need only look at the spirituality and culture of the time. If we wish, however, to know why people of the nineteenth century had a physical brain and an ether body suited to materialistic thinking, we must say that Halley's Comet appeared in 1835.

The so-called Enlightenment occurred in the eighteenth century. It marked a certain stage in the development of the human I. During the second half of the eighteenth century, the brain of the average person had a spiritual configuration called

6. Jakob Moleschott (1822–1893), author of *Der Kreislauf des Lebens* ("The Cycle of Life," 1852), and Ludwig Büchner (1824–1899), author of *Kraft und Stoff* ("Force and Matter," 1855).

"enlightenment." Goethe became angry at the fact that a few ideas were thrown around, and people declared themselves satisfied. But what created this brain for a so-called age of enlightenment? Halley's Comet created it in 1759. It was one of the comet's primary effects.

Every cometary body has a specific task. Human spiritual life advances with a certain cosmic regularity, as it were—a bourgeois regularity, one might say. Just as a person takes up certain daily activities with an earthly, bourgeois regularity—like lunch and dinner—so human spiritual life moves with cosmic regularity. And into this regularity come other events that, in ordinary bourgeois life, are out of the ordinary and through which a noticeable advance occurs. So it is, for example, when a child is born into a family. The cosmic regularity that manifests in human evolution as a whole moves along under the influence of the moon. In contrast to these events, there are occurrences that always lead to a step forward, and these are distributed over broader spans of time; these other events take place under the influence of comets.

The various comets have different tasks, and a comet splinters once it has served its purpose. Consequently, we find that, after a certain time, some comets appear as two and then splinter further. They dissolve once they have completed their tasks. All the regularity of the ordinary round of earthly life is connected with the lunar influence; the entry of an elemental impulse, which always incorporates something new, is related to the influence of comets. So we see that these seemingly erratic heavenly wanderers have their proper place and significance in the structure of our universe.

You can well imagine that, like an effect of the cosmic feminine, whenever something new breaks into human evolution, it can cause disturbances that are obvious enough, although people prefer not to notice. It is possible, however, to make people aware of the fact that certain earthly events are related to comets. Something new comes with comets, like a woman's gift that enters the normal routine of a family. When a comet returns, something new is produced, like the birth of a new child. Bear in mind, however, that certain comets always push the I further into the outer physical world, and this is something we must resist. If the influence of Halley's Comet were to continue, its next appearance might greatly enhance Büchnerian thought, and that would be very unfortunate. Be warned, therefore, that when Halley's Comet returns, it might prove to be an evil guest if we simply surrender to it and do not resist its influence. It is a matter of holding to higher and more significant cosmic activities and influences than those of Halley's Comet.

Nevertheless, people must consider this comet an omen and realize that things have changed since earlier times, when such influences were, in a sense, fruitful for humanity. This is no longer the case. To balance the harmful influence of Halley's Comet, people must now unite with different forces. It was said that this comet can be a warning—that its very influence might make people more superficial and push the human I increasingly into the physical world. I do not say this to revive an old superstition, but this is precisely the influences we must resist today. Such resistance can come only through a spiritual perspective of the world, such as anthroposophy, which can reverse the evolutionary trend helped by Halley's Comet.

It could be said that, once again, the Lord is displaying his staff there in the heavens, as though saying to humankind through this omen, "Now is the time to rekindle the life of spirit." On the other hand, isn't it wonderful that cometary existence takes hold in the depths of life, including the life of animals and plants as it relates to human life? Those who look closely enough at such things can see something very unusual in the blossoming of flowers. Such phenomena are present, but they are easily missed, just as people often overlook or do not wish to see the spirit.

Is there something in the cosmos that corresponds to the spiritual ascent just described? We have seen that head and limbs and male and female are polarities in the cosmos. Is there something in the cosmos that corresponds to this welling of the spirit—this advance of humankind beyond itself, from the lower self to the I?

We will ask this question tomorrow in connection with the greatest tasks of spiritual life today. Today I wanted to present the preliminaries, so that tomorrow, through larger relationships, we may understand an important question of our time. Much that has been said today is admittedly remote, but we are living in a cometary year, so it helps to say something about the mysterious relationship between cometary existence and our earthly existence. Beginning with this, tomorrow we will speak about the great spiritual meaning of our time.

5 · The Reappearance of Christ in the Etheric

Stuttgart, March 6, 1910

There is a connection between the past and the future in human evolution. Considering this helps us understand our task as human beings in any given period. When we gathered here some time ago, we spoke of the past in human evolution.[1] Today, we will discuss the connection between our past evolution and the immediate future. At the conclusion of yesterday's lecture, we pointed to an important indication that tells us, as if speaking from heaven, that humankind needs a new spiritual impulse. We cannot understand how this new impulse needs to work unless we consider the millennia just before Christianity and how it relates to the millennia after Christ—our own time.

There is a law that determines how certain events are repeated in human evolution, and we spoke of such repetitions in the previous lectures here in Stuttgart. Today I wish to point out in particular that, whenever spiritual science refers to such regular repetitions, do not think that you can establish them intellectually; repetitions must be examined in detail, after all,

---

1. Lectures on November 13 and 14, 1909; see *Die tieferen Geheimnisse des Menschheitswerdens im Lichte der Evangelien* (Rudolf Steiner Verlag, 1986; GA 117).

and verified by spiritual research. One can completely miss the point by using one repetition as a pattern to establish another. There is one repetition that does, in fact, resemble another: essential events that affected the time before Christianity were repeated in a certain way after the beginning of Christianity.

If we look at the three-thousand-year period just before Christianity appeared, we see that these three millennia are part of a historical epoch in human evolution called the lesser Dark Age, or Kali Yuga, which began in 3101 B.C. (This date is approximate, since human evolution moved along gradually.) All of what we think of today as the great achievements of humanity—the essential characteristic of human culture today—is related to this Dark Age. Before Kali Yuga, all human thinking and soul forces were, in a sense, still arranged differently. In the period before 3101 B.C., a residue of the old clairvoyance still existed. These periods follow one another in human evolution: Krita Yuga, Treta Yuga, Dvapara Yuga, Kali Yuga. The last one interests us today in particular. We arrive in old Atlantis during the earlier periods. Remnants of the old clairvoyance existed in ancient times, so that before the Kali Yuga, humankind retained the ability to see into the spirit world and, thus, a direct awareness of it.

Direct awareness of the spirit world gradually withdrew, and in general faculties and forces began to develop that limit human reason to the sensory world while, at the same time, cultivating human self-awareness. These forces began during Kali Yuga. Whereas people were no longer able to see into the spirit worlds, a firm point increasingly developed within the phenomenal world—the point we call knowledge, or I-being. Bear in mind, however, that human self-awareness was not yet very well developed but had to be further cultivated. It would never have entered human consciousness, however, if that Dark Age had not occurred. In the three millennia before Christianity, therefore, humankind gradually lost connection with the spirit world; people no longer had this connection through direct observation.

When I was here last, we saw how, at the end of the first millennium of Kali Yuga, a kind of compensation occurred for the lost ability to see into spirit worlds. This was given to human beings because a certain individual, Abraham, possessed an especially well-developed physical brain, through which he could become aware of the spirit world without the use of ancient faculties. In spiritual science, therefore, we call the first part of Kali Yuga the period of Abraham; human beings lost their direct sight into the higher spirit worlds, but, at the same time, something like an awareness of God also awakened in them. This gradually grew into I-awareness, so that people increasingly related the thought of God to I-being. The Godhead appeared as the universal I during that first thousand years of Kali Yuga, the end of which we may call the time of Abraham.

The age of Abraham was followed by the age of Moses, in which the God Jehovah, the universal I, no longer manifested as a mysterious guiding power in human destinies, but as the God of one race. We know that, during the age of Moses, the Godhead was revealed in the burning bush as the God of the elements. It was a tremendous advance when the universal I, the Godhead, was experienced through the teachings of Moses in such a way that one knew that the elements of existence (the phenomena of lightning, thunder, and so on) are, ultimately, emanations and activities of the universal cosmic-I.

We must be very clear about the extent to which this was real progress. Going back, beyond the age of Abraham and Kali

Yuga, we find that human beings saw spirit, because they retained remnants of the old clairvoyance and direct vision into the spirit worlds. We see this spiritual capacity in all ancient times. We must go back much farther in time to find something different. Human beings saw spirit during Dvapara Yuga, Treta Yuga, Krita Yuga. They saw spirit in such a way that it manifested as a myriad of beings. You know, of course, that when we ascend to the spirit worlds, we find hierarchies of spirit beings. They exist, as a matter of course, under a unified spiritual guidance. In those ancient times, however, consciousness did not reach as far as the unified spiritual guidance. One saw individual members of the hierarchies, or a multiplicity of divine beings. Only initiates could assemble them into a unity. Now, however, the human being was confronted by the universal I, first perceived through the physical instrument of the brain that was found especially in Abraham. Now humankind perceived manifestations of the universal I in the various kingdoms and elements of nature.

Then another advance occurred during the last millennium before Christianity, in the age of Solomon. We can therefore distinguish the three millennia before Christianity in this way: the first millennium is called the age of Abraham, after the one who appeared and affected the second. From the beginning of Kali Yuga until Abraham, human beings prepared themselves to recognize the one Godhead behind natural phenomena, and this possibility emerged with Abraham. In the age of Moses, the one God became the ruler of natural phenomena and was sought behind the phenomena of nature. All of this intensified during the age of Solomon. We are led through this age, up to the evolutionary point when the divine being, called Jehovah in the ages of Abraham and Moses, assumes human form.

In a spiritual scientific contemplation of this matter, we must stick to the fact that the Gospels are right about this: we cannot distinguish Christ from Jehovah, except in the sense that we distinguish direct sunlight from sunlight reflected by the moon. What sort of light do we have on a moonlit night? It is real sunlight, except that it is reflected to us from the moon. We receive sunlight directly during the day, whereas it is sent from the moon on moonlit nights. What we see in space in this way is presented also in time: the being who finally appeared as the Spirit Sun, the Christ, manifested earlier as a reflection. Jehovah is the reflection that precedes Christ in time. Just as moonlight is reflected sunlight, the Christ reflected himself for Abraham, Moses, and Solomon; it was always the same being. Then he appeared as the Christ Sun with the beginning of Christianity. Thus, the preparation for this great event took place during the ages of Abraham, Moses, and Solomon.

These three ages, as they occurred before the beginning of Christianity, are now repeated in the time following Christ, but in reverse. This repetition occurs in such a way that the essential feature of the Solomon age was repeated in the first millennium after Christ, and, indeed, the spirit of Solomon lives and weaves in the most outstanding spirits of the first Christian millennium. It was fundamentally the wisdom of Solomon through which people tried to comprehend the nature and essential character of the Christ event. The knowledge gained through Solomon's wisdom was used to understand the significance of the Christ event.

The next age can be called a revival of the Moses age. The repeated age of Solomon after Christ was followed by the age of Moses. During the second millennium after Christ, the spirit of Moses permeated the best people of the time. Indeed, we find this spirit of Moses revived in a new form. During pre-Christian times, the spirit of Moses looked out into the world, toward natural phenomena, to find the universal I, the Godhead as Jehovah, in thunder and lightning and all that can flow into human beings as the great law of human action. Just as the universal I flowed into Moses as revealed externally, so to speak, we find that, during the second age after Christ, that same being is proclaimed within the human soul. For Moses, that impression was an outer event, as when he withdrew from his people to receive the Ten Commandments. This significant event was repeated during the second millennium after Christ through a powerful inner revelation. Things are not repeated in exactly the same way, but as a kind of polarity. Consequently, if God revealed himself to Moses through the elements of nature, he revealed himself from the deepest foundations of the human soul during the second millennium after Christ.

How could this come to us in a more sublime way than to hear of a remarkable man of lofty talents who preaches about profound matters from the depths of his soul? We can assume that this preacher was deeply imbued with what we call mystical Christianity. Then a seemingly insignificant layman came to where he preached and began to listen to his sermons. Later, however, it turned out that he was no layman, and even became Tauler's instructor.[2] Although he had attained such a

---

2. Johannes Tauler (c. 1300–1361), German mystic and Dominican. While studying, he met Meister Eckhart in Strasbourg and became one of his disciples. Because the churches of Strasbourg were closed by the bishop there as the result of a quarrel between Pope John XXII and Emperor Louis IV, Tauler went to Basel, where he associated with leaders of the Friends of God, a popular mystical movement that spread Eckhart's teachings. See Rudolf Steiner, *Mystics after Modernism: Discovering the Seeds of a New Science in the Renaissance* (Anthroposophic Press, 2000; GA 7).

lofty level, the preacher Tauler suspended his preaching until he felt permeated by what lived in that "layman." After opening himself to this inspiration, Tauler again ascended the pulpit, and the powerful impression of his sermon is made clear to us symbolically when we hear that many of his listeners fell to the ground as though they had died. In other words, everything of a lower nature within them had been killed. It was a revelation of the universal I, working just as powerfully from within as it had with Moses through the elements during that second pre-Christian age. So we see the age of Moses reborn in such a way that its spirit permeated and radiated life into the whole spirit of Christian mysticism, from Meister Eckhart to the later Christian mystics. The spirit of Moses truly lived in these Christian mystics; it was present in such a way that it entered and animated their souls.

That was the second age following Christ, when the whole character of the age of Moses was resurrected. During the first millennium of the Christian era, the second age of Solomon shaped the Christian view and, for example, all that we know as the hierarchies in the Christian sense; in a way, it detailed the wisdom of the higher worlds. Likewise, the second age of Moses gave form to what became German mysticism—the deep, mystical consciousness of the one God, who can be reborn in the human soul. This age of Moses has continued, since that time, to affect all efforts to investigate more exactly the universal I and one God.

In keeping with the course of human evolution, a renewal of the age of Abraham is beginning in our time, during which we will pass gradually into the third millennium. Just as the age of Abraham was followed by that of Solomon in pre-Christian times, so they appear in reverse order during the Christian era—the ages of Solomon, Moses, and Abraham. We are currently moving toward the new age of Abraham, and it will bring powerful events.

Let us consider the significance of Abraham's time. The old clairvoyance had vanished, and humankind was given a consciousness of God closely connected with human faculties. Everything that humanity could acquire from this consciousness, which is bound to the human brain, has gradually drained away, and in fact little remains to be acquired through these human faculties. On the contrary, we are headed in exactly the opposite direction during the new age of Abraham. We are taking a path that will lead humanity away from merely physical, sensory contemplation and reason. We are going along a path that will lead humankind back to where it was before the age of Abraham. We are going along a path that leads to conditions of natural clairvoyance. In the age of Kali Yuga, only initiation could lead us appropriately into spirit worlds. Initiation leads to higher levels, which human beings will not be able to attain naturally until the distant future. Nevertheless, the first traces of renewed clairvoyance—which will become a natural human capacity—will manifest fairly soon as we pass into the new age of Abraham.

After we have won self-awareness and have come to know that our I-being is a firm central point in our inner being, we will again be guided outward to look more deeply into spirit worlds. This is still connected with that age when Kali Yuga ended. It lasted 5,000 years, until 1899, which was indeed an important year for human evolution. This again is an approximate year, since such events happen gradually. We can designate 3101 B.C. as the year humanity was led down from the old clairvoyance to sensory perception and intellectual reason;

similarly, in 1899 humanity received another sudden thrust forward, thus beginning an ascent to future human clairvoyance. It is allotted to humanity to develop the first elements of a new clairvoyance before the twenty-first century and, for a few, even during the first half of the twentieth century. This clairvoyance will most certainly appear in humanity once people have proved capable of understanding it.

We must clearly understand that there are two possibilities. It is inherent in the essential nature of the human soul that, during the first half of the twentieth century, a few people will attain natural clairvoyant faculties (we must differentiate between cultivated and natural clairvoyance). But if people have the will, these numbers will increase during the next 2,500 years, until enough people will have finally attained this new, natural clairvoyance.

One possibility is that people will have an aptitude for clairvoyance, but materialism will triumph during the coming decades, and humanity will sink into a materialistic swamp. A few rare people will appear who say that it seems they saw something like a second being in the physical human being. Yet, if materialistic consciousness reaches the point of viewing spiritual science as a folly and stamping out all consciousness of spirit worlds, people will simply fail to understand these seminal capacities. It will depend on humanity itself whether these events turn out to be a blessing or a curse, since it may pass by unnoticed.

There is another possibility, however, in which spiritual science does not get trampled. When these faculties appear toward the middle of the twentieth century, people will understand that such qualities should not only be cultivated in secret schools of initiation, but that they should also be cherished as the delicate seedlings of human soul life. As though from an awakened soul force, such people will see the reality of the second being within the physical human being, just as spiritual science describes it. Other faculties will also appear that people will become aware of in themselves. For example, when they do something and then look up from their activity, something like a dream image will appear before their souls, and they will recognize that it is connected with their action. People will know, on the basis of spiritual science, that when an action's after-image appears—though essentially different from the action—it must show the karmic effect of the action as it will appear in the future.

A few people will have this kind of karmic understanding by the middle of the twentieth century, because Kali Yuga has run its course and, with each epoch, new human faculties appear. It will be a disaster for humankind, however, if understanding is not created—if this faculty is trampled to death, as it were, and those who speak of these capacities are considered crazy and locked up; humanity will decay in a swamp of materialism. This all depends on whether an understanding awakens for spiritual science, or the backward, materialistic current of Ahriman succeeds in resisting the beneficial effects of spiritual science. We can be sure that those who become mired and choke in the swamp of materialism will jeer, "Yes, indeed, those were fine prophets who said that people would see a second being with the physical human being." Certainly, nothing will manifest if the necessary faculties have been trampled to death. If these faculties do not become apparent by the middle of the twentieth century, however, it will not prove that human beings do not have such a capacity, but that they have trampled the budding young shoots. What has been described today is present and can be developed if people will it.

So we see that we are living amid important, essential conditions in our age, and we know that the task of disseminating spiritual science today is not done by preference but required by time in which we live. To prepare humanity for great moments in evolution is one task of spiritual research. Spiritual science exists so that people will recognize what they see. Those who are true to the age in which they live cannot help but think that spiritual knowledge must come into the world, so that what the future brings does not to go unnoticed by humanity. Therefore, we face evolution directly, and we retrace our steps, as it were, along the path of evolution. With Abraham, our awareness of God was led into the brain; as we enter the new age of Abraham, this cognition of God is, in turn, led out of the brain and, during the next 2,500 years, we will gradually recognize those who will will possess the exalted secrets of initiation, the great spiritual teachings of cosmic mysteries.

The spirit of Moses ruled the age that has now run its course; now the spirit of Abraham begins to rule, so that, having led humanity to awareness of God within the sensory world, he can now lead humanity out again. It is an eternal cosmic law that every individual must perform a certain act repeatedly. We must, above all, perform it twice, the second time as though doing the opposite of the first. Abraham brought something into physical consciousness for humanity that he will return to the spiritual world for humanity.

These matters are connected with still others. In certain other ways, everything renews itself in such repetitions. We are approaching a time when even more of what existed in the pre-Christian centuries will be renewed for humanity, but everything will be immersed in what humanity has been able to win through the great Christ event. We have seen that humanity has now experienced again, in an esoteric Christian way, Moses' great moment when he experienced the burning bush and fiery flash on Sinai. The Taulers and the Eckharts of today know clearly that, when the being whom Moses called Jehovah arises within them, it is the Christ. But now it is no longer the reflected Christ, but the Christ himself who rises from the depths of one's heart. Moses' experience was, in fact, met again by Christian mystics, but in a Christian form, altered by the Christ impulse. Those experiences during the pre-Christian time of Abraham will be experienced in a completely different and new form. What will this form be? All phenomena and events that appear normally in human evolution cast their lights ahead, as it were. (I do not wish to use the cliché "cast their shadows," but rather "cast their lights.") Thus, in a certain sense, something related to events of the future is cast ahead in light, as Saul's conversion to Paul near Damascus.

Let us become clear about what this event meant for Paul. Until that event, Paul was familiar with everything involved in the old esoteric Hebrew doctrine. What did Paul know? He knew, through the ancient Hebrew esotericism, that one day an individual would descend to earth and represent for humanity the one who would overcome death. He knew that an individual would appear one time in the flesh. Through his life, that one would demonstrate that the spirit continues beyond death, so that death would mean only another physical event for that one in his earthly incarnation. Paul knew this. He also knew from the ancient esoteric doctrine of the Hebrews that the spiritual sphere of earth would be transformed when the Christ, the Messiah who was to come, had presented himself in the flesh, when he had risen from the dead and had won a victory over death.

Clairvoyance itself would be transformed. Previously, a clairvoyant could not see the Christ being in the spiritual atmosphere of the earth, but only when looking to the Sun Spirit. Paul knew, however, that, through the Christ impulse, earthly existence must be transformed—that after the Christ's victory over death, the Christ would be found by clairvoyant consciousness in the earthly sphere. Consequently, those who become clairvoyant must see the Christ in the earthly sphere as the active Earth Spirit. While he was still Saul, however, Paul had remained unconvinced that the one who lived in Palestine and died on the cross, and the one whose disciples claimed had risen from the dead, was in fact the one spoken of by ancient Hebraic esoteric doctrine. The important thing is that, through what he had seen physically, Paul became convinced of what the Gospels relate. He gained the conviction that Christ was the predicted Messiah only when that event cast its forward-directed light in him—when he became clairvoyant through grace and discovered the Christ in the earthly sphere.

Paul must have said to himself, "He has already been here and risen from the dead." Once Paul had seen the Christ clairvoyantly in the spiritual sphere of the earth, he knew that the Christ had been present. From that moment on, he was completely convinced of Jesus the Christ. The essential event, therefore, was that, through what happened near Damascus, he found Jesus Christ clairvoyantly in the earthly sphere. If Paul had been unable to hear the accounts in Palestine of the activities of Jesus Christ, if he had not been able to personally experience the Gospels but had lived somewhat later, he might have simply experienced this Christ event near Damascus later on. He would have nevertheless arrived at the same conviction, because it revealed to him that the Christ was present. The one who reveals himself in the earthly sphere is the one spoken of by the ancient esoteric Hebrew doctrine.

The Christ event is not limited to only one point in time. For Paul, it simply followed soon after so that Christianity could pursue its course through him. Of course, during the following time of Kali Yuga until 1899, humanity had not developed in such a way that a person could simply experience an event such as Paul's; human faculties had not ripened sufficiently. It could, however, be experienced by grace, and others also experienced such events through grace. We now live, however, in a time when this powerful and revolutionary change is about to occur, and the first seeds of natural clairvoyance will evolve. We are entering the age of Abraham and being led out into the spiritual world. As a result, a certain number of human beings—and during the next 2,500 years more and more—will be given the possibility of repeating Paul's experience near Damascus. The greatness and power of the next age will lie in the fact that the event of Damascus will come to life for many people. Through the faculties I have described, the Christ will become perceptible in the spiritual sphere of the earth; he will radiate into these faculties. As people become increasingly able to see the ether body, they will come to see the ether body of Jesus Christ, even as Paul saw it.

This is now beginning as a characteristic of the new age, and it will manifest between 1930 and 1945, at first among human beings who will possess such faculties. If people pay attention, they will experience this event of Damascus through direct spiritual observation and, with it, become clear about the truth of the Christ event.

Striking parallels will take place, because in the next two decades human beings will gradually fall away from the letter of the Gospels and no longer understand them. Even today, we see superficial scholars everywhere "proving" that the Gospels are not history and that we cannot speak of a historic Christ. These historical documents will lose their value for humanity; those who deny Jesus Christ will become greater in number. Short-sighted people will still be able to believe that Christianity can be saved by a mere story. Those whose intentions are honest toward Christianity do not refuse to understand the spiritual proof of Jesus Christ. The spiritual proof of Jesus Christ will come by nurturing the human faculties through which they will see the truly existing Christ in his ether body. After all, no matter how much those who call themselves good Christians choose to rely only on documents, they nevertheless destroy Christianity. No matter how much they raise a fuss and loudly proclaim how they understand Christianity through docu-ments, they are still destroying Christianity. They destroy it because they reject the spiritual teaching that tells us Christ will become truth for human beings through vision in our century.

When our era began, human beings had been descending into the Dark Age for more than three thousand years, and they depended on their outer faculties. At that time, physical incarnation was the only way Christ could reveal himself to the faculties that were necessary for human evolution. The physical faculties had reached the peak of development, and Christ had to appear in a physical body. Humanity would not have advanced another step, however, if it would not become possi-ble to find the reality of Christ in higher worlds through higher faculties. Just as Christ had to be found with purely physical faculties then, human beings will use newly developed faculties to find Christ in a world where only ether bodies are seen; there will be no second physical incarnation of Christ. He appeared only once in the flesh, because only then did human faculties depend on seeing Christ in a physical body. Now, however, with the development of higher faculties, human beings will perceive the far more real ether body of the Christ.

This is how we can describe the reappearance of Jesus Christ, the powerful, gradual event that lies ahead of us—for only a few to begin with, and, over time, for more and more. Some who are now incarnated will still be on earth when the next Christ event takes place, but it will be significant for more than those who will still be incarnated in the flesh. People will experience it as it has been described, and others will have gone through the portal of death. We once learned here that the event of Golgotha was not only for the physical world, but its effects carried into all spirit worlds—just as the descent of Christ into the underworld was a concrete fact. Similarly, the Christ event of the twentieth century will also affect the world between death and a new birth, although in a different way for those on earth. One thing will be needed, however; the faculties required for perceiving the Christ event between death and a new birth cannot be acquired there, but must be developed here on the physical plane and taken into one's life between death and a new birth.

We are placed on the physical earth for a purpose, since there are faculties we must acquire on earth. Anyone who thinks we were put on earth for no reason is on the wrong track. We must acquire faculties here that cannot be acquired in any other world. The capacity for an understanding of the Christ event we have described, as well as the events that follow, must be acquired on earth. Those who acquire these capacities here and now on earth through the teachings of spiritual science will carry them through the portal of death. One acquires these faculties not only through initiation, but also by understanding and accepting of the teachings of spiritual science, thus gaining the possibility of perceiving the Christ event, even in the spiritual world between death and a new birth. Those who remain deaf to this, however, will have to wait for another incarnation to acquire the faculties we must acquire here, otherwise one will be unable to experience the Christ event in the spiritual world. Consequently, no one should believe that those who die before this event will not reap the fruits revealed by this Christ event, which is comprehensible only through the insights of spiritual science; it will indeed bear fruit for them.

Thus, we see that spiritual research prepares us for the new Christ event. By taking in the essence of spiritual teachings and filling our souls with its vitality, we can grow upward to a spiritual understanding of this matter. People should be aware that they must thoroughly understand our newly awakening age through spiritual science. We must come to understand that, in the future, we cannot look to the physical world for the most important events, but beyond it; we will have to look for Christ's return in an etheric form within the spirit world.

What has been described will be repeated again and again in the coming decades. Some will misunderstand this, however, and say, "The Christ will return." Since such ideas will involve belief in a physical return, they will encourage the appearance of false messiahs. There will be many such individuals in the mid-twentieth century, and they will use people's materialistic beliefs to pass themselves off as the Christ. There have always been false messiahs. During the age before the Crusades, for example, a false messiah appeared in the south of France, whose followers saw something in him that seemed like Christ incarnated in a physical body. Earlier, a false messiah appeared in Spain and had many followers. In North Africa, an individual presented himself as the Christ and created a great sensation. During the seventeenth century, a man appeared in Smyrna as Christ and gained a large following. This was Shabattai Tzevi (1626–1675). People made pilgrimages to see him, coming from Poland, Hungary, Austria, Spain, Germany, France—from all of Europe and much of Africa and Asia.

During those centuries, this was not so terrible, because people were not yet required to distinguish the true from the false. Only now do we live in an age when it would be a disaster if people fail to pass this spiritual test. People have to realize that human faculties must continue to evolve. The faculties needed to see Christ in a physical body could perceive him only at the beginning of Christianity, and humanity will not have advanced if the Christ is not perceived in a higher form during our century. Those who strive for spiritual science will have to prove able to distinguish false messiahs from the true messiah, who will appear not in the flesh but as a spirit to newly awakened faculties.

The time will come when human beings will again look into the spirit world and see the land from which streams flow down and give real spiritual nourishment to everything in the physical world. We have, in fact, always seen that it is possible for those endowed with the old clairvoyance to see into the spirit world. Eastern scriptures traditionally contain something like a record handed down that tells of an ancient spirit land, which human beings were once able to see. From that land, they were able draw all that flows into the physical world from the suprasensory realm. Many descriptions, full of melancholy, describe that land—one that people were once able to reach but now seems to have withdrawn. This land was indeed accessible to human beings, and it will be accessible again, now that Kali Yuga has run its course.

Initiation always led into that mysterious land, but it is spoken of now as a country that vanished from the sphere of human experience. It withdrew during Kali Yuga, but for those who received initiation, it has always been possible to guide their way into it. The stories of this ancient country are touching. Initiates repeatedly went to that land to receive the new streams and impulses that had to be given to humanity from century to century. Again and again, those who bear this relationship to the spirit world enter that mysterious land. It is called Shambhala, the primal fountainhead that clairvoyant sight once penetrated, but then withdrew during Kali Yuga. It is spoken of as one would speak of an ancient fairyland—one that will nevertheless return to the human realm. Shambhala will be present again now that Kali Yuga has run its course. Through normal human faculties, humankind will again advance into Shambhala, the land from which initiates derive strength and wisdom for their mission. Shambhala is present, just as it always was and will be again for humanity. When Shambhala reveals itself again, one of the first visions people will have will be of Christ in his etheric form. Humanity has no leader but Christ as a guide into this land that vanished according to writings of the East. Christ will lead humanity to Shambhala.

We must inscribe this into our souls. It can happen for humanity if we correctly interpret the omen of Halley's Comet, which we have discussed. Humanity needs to understand that it must not sink deeper into matter, but must reverse its course. A spiritual life must begin, so that Shambhala will arise— woven and gleaming with light, abounding with life, and filling our hearts with wisdom. At first this will occur for only a few, then, during the next 2,500 years, for more and more people. For those with the desire to understand, and for those with ears to hear and eyes to see, this event must be described as the greatest turning point in human evolution, occurring at the dawn of the new age of Abraham. Through this event, humankind will better understand the Christ impulse. Through the unique nature of this event, wisdom will not be lost. The power of Christ's appearance will increase as more and more people gain the ability to see him.

Once people are able to penetrate Shambhala with their vision, they will also be able to understand the real meaning of much that is contained in the Gospels. If we are to truly acknowledge what is given in the Gospels, we need a kind of event of Damascus. Thus, at a time when people have the least confidence in those documents, a new profession of faith in Jesus Christ will arise as we grow into the sphere where we shall encounter him—in the mysterious land of Shambhala.

6 · The Sermon on the Mount and the Land of Shambhala

München, March 15, 1910

Previously we discussed the present point in time and how humankind is confronted by difficult events. We will better understand the reason for this if we consider our time retrospectively by looking at human evolution as a whole, thus bringing ourselves up to date on many matters, both known and unknown. You know that one of the most significant pronouncements made as the Christ event approached was, "Change the disposition of your souls, for the kingdom of heaven is at hand" (Matt. 3:2). These words are deeply meaningful, indicating that something very significant was taking place then for the whole of human soul development. When these words were spoken, it had been more than three thousand years since the beginning of what we call Kali Yuga, the Dark Age. What is the significance of this age? During that era, it was normal for people to depend solely on the outer senses for perception, as well as the kind of understanding that uses the brain as its instrument. This was all that could be experienced, known, and understood in the dark age of Kali Yuga.

This Dark Age was preceded by an age when human beings did not depend only upon the physical senses and intellect.

They more or less retained a memory of an ancient dreamlike condition, whereby they could experience a connection with the spirit world. It is of those ancient human times that we want to picture.

People then saw not only the mineral, plant, and animal realms, as well as themselves within the physical, human realm, but also, in the state between waking and sleeping, they could see a divine world. The viewed themselves as the lowest members of the lowest of the hierarchies. Above them were the angels, archangels, and so on. The knew this through their own experience, therefore it would have been absurd to deny the existence of a spirit world, just as today it would be absurd to deny the existence of mineral, plant, and animal realms. Not only were they aware of the wisdom that flowed toward humankind from spirit realms, but they also had the capacity to become completely imbued with the forces from that world. They would go into a state of ecstasy, and, although the sense of I-being was submerged, the spirit world and its forms flowed into them. Consequently, they not only gained knowledge and experience of the spirit world, but, when ill, for example, they could also be healed and refreshed through their ecstasy.

Eastern wisdom refers to the ages when humankind still had a direct connection with the spirit world as Krita Yuga, Treta Yuga, and Dvapara Yuga. In the most recent age, however, direct sight into the spirit world was no longer possible and became only a memory, just as an old man might recall his youth. When the doors to the spirit worlds closed, people could no longer visit those realms in a normal state of consciousness, and the time came when a long, rigorous training in the mystery schools was required before one could turn again toward the spirit world.

During Kali Yuga, however, the spirit realms did occasionally penetrate into the physical world. As a rule, this did not originate from benevolent powers, but more often those of a demonic nature. The strange illnesses described in the Gospels, in which people were said to be possessed, can be attributed to demonic forces. Here we must recognize the influence of spirit beings. This lesser Kali Yuga began around 3000 B.C. and is characterized by the fact that the doors to the spirit world gradually closed completely to normal human consciousness, so that all knowledge must come from the sensory world. If this process had continued, any possible connection with the spiritual world would have been lost to humankind. Until the time of Kali Yuga, human beings were able to recall certain truths preserved by tradition, but today even these connections have faded. Even teachers, the preservers of tradition, could not speak to people directly about spirit worlds, because the necessary receptivity no longer existed. Human knowledge was gradually limited to the phenomenal world.

If this development had continued, human beings would never again be able to find a connection with the spiritual world, regardless of how we might try; our connection would have been lost if something had not occurred from another direction: the physical embodiment of the divine being whom we call the Christ.

In previous times, people had been able to lift themselves to spirit beings, but now spirit had to approach humankind and descend fully into this realm, whereby we would be able to recognize spirit through our own essence, the I. This moment had been prophesied in ancient times. It was said that human beings would be able to regain their relationship to God within their I-being. But when this time came, it had to be brought forcefully to the attention of humanity that the promised moment had in fact arrived. The one who announced this event most powerfully was John the Baptist. He announced that the times had changed, saying, "The kingdom of heaven is at hand" (Matt. 3:2). Later this was said in a similar way by Jesus Christ (Matt. 4:17). The most significant sign, however, was given in advance through the many baptisms performed by John in the Jordan and through the teaching itself.

Nevertheless, by those means alone, real change would not have been possible. Some would have needed a much more significant experience of the spirit world to become convinced that a divine being would be revealed. This was accomplished by submerging them in water. When a person is about to drown, the connection between the ether body and the physical body is loosened—the ether body withdraws somewhat—and in this way a person can experience an indication of that new impulse in world evolution. From this arises the powerful admonition: Change the disposition of your soul, for the kingdoms of heaven are near. The disposition of your soul is upon you, through which you will find a relationship to the descended Christ. The times have been fulfilled.

Jesus Christ expressed the fulfillment of the times in the penetrating teachings in his "Sermon on the Mount," as it is called. This was certainly not a sermon for the masses. The Gospels read, "When Christ saw the multitudes of people, He withdrew from them and revealed Himself to His disciples" (Matt. 5:1–2). He revealed to them that, in ancient times, people could become filled with God during ecstasy. While outside their I-being, they became blissful and had direct experience of the spirit world, from which they could draw spiritual and healing forces. Jesus Christ told his disciples that now people can be filled with God by permeating themselves with the God and Christ impulse and by uniting their I-being with it. In the past, no one could ascend to the spiritual world who was not filled with streams from the spirit world. One had to be rich in the spirit to be called blessed. Such people were clairvoyant in the old sense, and they were rare. Most people had become beggars for the spirit. Now, those who sought the kingdom of heaven could find it through their I.

The events of such a significant human epoch always affects all of humankind. If one member of one's being is touched, the others respond; all the members of the human being—the physical and ether bodies, the sentient, rational, and consciousness souls, the I, and even the higher members of the soul—received new life because the kingdom of heaven was near. These teachings are in complete harmony with the great wisdom teachings of primeval times.

To enter the spirit world in earlier times, the ether body had to be separated slightly from the physical body, which was thus formed in a special way. Jesus Christ therefore said, alluding to the physical body: Blessed are the beggars—the poor in spirit—for if, through the I, they develop their outer bodies correctly, they will find the kingdom of heaven (Matt. 5:3). He said of the etheric body: Formerly, people could be healed of illnesses in the body and soul by rising into the spirit world in a state of ecstasy. Now, those who suffer and are filled with the spirit of God can be healed and comforted, and they can find the source, the comfort, within themselves (Matt. 5:4). He said of the astral body: In former times those whose astral bodies were beset by wild and tempestuous passions and impulses could be subdued only when equanimity, peace, and purification streamed to them from divine spirit beings. Now, however, human beings should find the strength within their I-being, under the influence of Christ, to purify their astral bodies. The place in which the astral body can be purified is now the earth. Thus the new influence in the astral body had to be presented by saying, Blessed and filled in their astral bodies with God are those who foster calmness and equanimity within themselves; all comfort and well-being on earth shall be their reward (Matt. 5:5).

The fourth Beatitude refers to the sentient soul. Those who thoroughly purify themselves in their sentient soul and gain a higher development will receive a hint of the Christ in their I. In their hearts, they will notice a thirst for righteousness; they will be pervaded with godliness, and the I-being will become sufficient unto itself (Matt 5:6).

The next member is the rational, mind soul. In the sentient soul, the I sleeps; it awakens only in the rational or feeling soul. If we slumber with our I in the sentient soul, we cannot find the true human being in others: I-being. Before we have developed the I within us, we must allow our sentient soul to grow into higher worlds so that it can perceive something there. When we have developed ourselves in our rational, mind soul, however, we can truly perceive another person.

As far as the other members of the human being are concerned, we must bear in mind what they received in earlier realms. It is only the mind soul that can fill itself with what flows between human beings. In the fifth Beatitude, the sentence structure will have to take on a special form. The subject and the predicate must be alike, since it concerns something that the I develops within itself. The fifth Beatitude says, Those who develop compassion and mercy shall find compassion in others (Matt. 5:7). This is a "cross-test," indicating that we are here dealing with an occult document. Christ has promised everything, harmonized everything, according to the individual members of the human being.

The next sentence of the Beatitudes refers to the consciousness soul. Through this member, I-being is purified and becomes capable of receiving God into itself. If we can lift ourselves enough in this way, we can perceive within ourselves that drop of the divine, the universal I; through purified consciousness soul, we can see God. This sixth sentence of the Beatitudes must, therefore, refer to seeing God. The outer physical expression for I-being and the consciousness soul is the physical blood, and where it expresses itself most particularly is in the human heart, as an expression of purified I-being. Christ said, therefore, Blessed are the pure in heart, for they shall behold God (Matt. 5:8). We are shown how, in the most intimate sense, the heart is the expression of I-being, the divine nature of human beings.

Now let us advance higher than the consciousness soul, to *manas, buddhi,* and *atman.*[1] Contemporary humankind may well cultivate the three lower members of the soul, but not until the distant future will we be able to develop these higher members: spirit self, life spirit, and spirit body. These cannot yet live in human beings; for this to occur we must be able to look to higher beings. Our spirit self is not yet within us; it will flow into us later. Human beings have not yet evolved enough to receive the spirit self fully into themselves. In this sense, we are at the beginning of our development; we are vessels that will receive it gradually. This is indicated in the seventh Beatitude. At first, the spirit self can only weave into human beings and fill them with its warmth. It is being brought down to

---

1. See Rudolf Steiner, *Theosophy* (Anthroposophic Press, 1994), pp. 50–62.

earth as the power of love and harmony because of the act of Christ. Therefore, Christ says, Blessed are those who draw the spirit self, the first spiritual member, down into themselves, for they shall become the children of God (Matt. 5:9). This points humankind upward to higher worlds.

Further on, he mentions what will be brought about in the future, but it will encounter increasing opposition in the present time and be fiercely rejected. This is indicated in the eighth Beatitude: Filled with God, or blessed, are they who are persecuted for righteousness sake, for they will be fulfilled in themselves with the kingdom of heaven, with life spirit, or buddhi (Matt. 5:10). In connection with this, we also find references to the special mission of Christ himself: Christ's intimate disciples may consider themselves blessed if they must suffer persecution for his sake (Matt. 5:11). This is a vague allusion to spirit body, or atman, which will be imparted to us in the distant future.

In the Sermon on the Mount, therefore, the great message is proclaimed: The kingdom of heaven is at hand. In the course of these events, the mystery of human evolution was fulfilled in Palestine. Human beings had reached a degree of maturity in all the members of the body, so that they were able, with their purified physical forces, to receive the Christ impulse directly into themselves. Thus it happened that Christ, the divine being, merged with Jesus of Nazareth, the human being, and for three years they imbued the earth with their joined forces. This had to happen so that human beings would not lose completely their connection to the spirit world during Kali Yuga.

Kali Yuga, however, continued until 1899. This was a particularly important year in human evolution, because it marked the end of the 5,000-year period of Kali Yuga and the beginning of a new stage in human evolution. In addition to the old faculties present during Kali Yuga, humankind would now develop new spiritual faculties. Thus we are approaching a period when new natural faculties and possibilities for looking into the divine spirit worlds will awaken. Before the first half of the twentieth century has passed, some people will, with full I-awareness, witness the penetration of the divine spirit world into the physical, sensory world, just as Saul did during his transformation into Paul near Damascus. This will become the normal condition for some people.

Christ will not incarnate again in a physical body as he did at the time of Jesus; nothing could be accomplished in this way. It was necessary then because of profound laws of cosmic and earthly evolution; otherwise, people would not have been able to recognize the Christ. Now, however, human beings have evolved and become capable of penetrating the etheric world through their soul forces. Christ will become visible to human beings in an ether body, not a physical body. For the next 2,500 years, from the mid-twentieth century on, this will become increasingly common. By then, enough people will have had experiences like that of Paul near Damascus that it will be assumed common on the earth.

We are involved with spiritual science so that these new faculties (at first barely perceptible) will not be overlooked and lost by humanity—so that those who are blessed with this new power of vision will not be seen as dreamers and fools, but instead receive support and understanding from a small group of people who, in their common purpose, may prevent these delicate soul seeds and qualities from being roughly trampled to death for lack of understanding. Spiritual science will indeed prepare the way for attaining this ability. I have explained before that these new qualities give us an insight into the land of Shambhala, through which we can come to know the true significance and nature of Christ, whose second coming indicates the maturation of human cognition.

In general, historical ages repeat, but always in a new way. In spiritual science, the beginning of Kali Yuga is seen as the closing of the portals to the spiritual world. After the first thousand years of Kali Yuga had passed, the first compensation for that loss occurred: in Abraham, after his initiation by Melchizedek, it became possible for a human being to recognize God in the outer world through true insight and a proper evaluation of the outer world—a world spread out, as it were, like a carpet before one's senses. With Abraham, we see the first knowledge of an "I-God," a God related to human I-being. Abraham realized that, behind the phenomenal world of the senses, there is something that made it possible for the human I to conceive itself as a drop of the infinite, unfathomable cosmic I.

A second state of this revelation of God was experienced in the time of Moses, when God approached humankind through the elements. In the burning bush and the thunder and lightning upon Sinai, he revealed himself to human senses and spoke to the innermost human being. A third millennium followed, when knowledge of God penetrated humankind. This was the age of Solomon, in which God revealed himself through the symbols of the temple that Solomon built in Jerusalem. The divine revelation thus proceeded in stages. God first appeared to Abraham as the I-God, Jehovah, then to Moses as fire in the burning bush, in thunder and lightning, and then to Solomon in the symbols of the Temple.

The qualities that represent a particular age are repeated later in reverse. The turning point is the appearance of Jesus Christ in Palestine. The qualities immediately preceding that time are the first to reappear. Consequently, the first millennium after Christ is a new Solomon epoch; the spirit of Solomon worked in the best human beings of that time so that the Mystery of Golgotha could penetrate. In those early centuries after Christ, Solomon's symbols could be interpreted most readily and inwardly by those who were able to experience most deeply the act on Golgotha.

In the second millennium after Christ we recognize a repetition of the age of Moses. What Moses experienced outwardly now appears in the mysticism of those such as Eckhart, Tauler, and so on. Those mystics experienced within what Moses experienced outwardly in the burning bush and in the thunder and lightning. They spoke of how the I-God revealed himself to them when they withdrew into themselves. When they perceived within their souls the spark of I-being, then the I-God, the one God Jehovah, revealed himself. This was true of Tauler, who was a great preacher and could experience powerful revelations. The layman called "The Friend of God from the Mountain" came to him, and people assumed he wanted to become Tauler's pupil. But instead he soon became Tauler's teacher, after which Tauler was able to speak of God from his inner being with such force that some were said to have fallen, lying as though dead, as he preached. This is reminiscent of events when Moses received the laws on Sinai.

The centuries leading up to our time have been filled with this spirit. Now, however, we are entering an era that recalls the age of Abraham, but now in the sense that human beings are led away from the sensory world. The spirit of Abraham will influence our knowledge so that human beings will renounce the old mentality that acknowledged only the sensory realm.

However, in contrast to Abraham (for whom the spirit of God could be found only in the sensory world), we will grow beyond the phenomenal world into the spirit world.

Human beings must not believe that Christ will reappear in the flesh, as some false teachings claim. If that were to happen, it would be impossible to believe in the evolution of human faculties, and we would have to say that events repeat in exactly the same way. This is not how it works, however; events do repeat, but on higher levels each time. Although people knew nothing of all this in the past, one would have to say that this has not interfered with our evolution. In the era now approaching, however, people will be placed in situations that will require them to assume conscious responsibility for their destinies. They must understand how Christ will be seen in the future.

The legend is true that, after the event of Golgotha, Christ descended to be with the dead in the spirit world so that he could bring them the message of salvation. The Christ event works in the same way today. It is thus the same, whether a person lives in the physical world here on earth or has passed through death. If we have gained an understanding for the Christ event here on earth, we will be able to experience it in the spiritual world. This demonstrates the fact that humankind has lived on this earth for a good reason. However, those who fail to acquire an understanding of the Christ event on earth will not, between death and a new birth, experience any trace of the effects of that event on Golgotha. They will have to wait until they return to earth and a new birth to prepare themselves.

In the coming centuries, there will be frequent claims of Christ's return to reveal himself. False messiahs and false Christs will appear. However, those who understand what was

just said about Christ's true appearance will reject such manifestations. Those who know can see the history of the last centuries in this light and will not be astonished or exalted by the
appearance of false messiahs. There were examples of this just
before the Crusades, as well as during the seventeenth century,
when the false messiah Shabattai Tzevi appeared in Smyrna.
Pilgrims flocked came from as far as France and Spain.

At that time, such a deception did not do very much harm.
Now, however, people possess more advanced faculties and
should realize that he will reappear in the ether body. People
should be able to recognize such a mistake and not believe that
Christ will come again in the flesh. Today, it is necessary to
clearly distinguish such things; confusion will have serious consequences. A "Christ" who reappears in the flesh should not be
trusted—only the Christ who appears in an ether body. This
appearance will take the form of a natural initiation, just as initiates now experience this event in a particular way.

We are approaching an age when people will feel they are
surrounded not only by a physical, sensory world, but also—
according to their understanding—by a spiritual kingdom.
The leader in this new kingdom of spirit will be the etheric
Christ. No matter what religious community or faith people
belong to, once they experience these facts within themselves,
they will acknowledge and accept the Christ event. Christians
who experience the etheric Christ are perhaps in a more difficult situation than adherents to other religions, yet they should
try to accept this Christ event with no more bias than they
would any other. It will, in fact, be our task to develop, especially through Christianity, an understanding for the possibility
of entering the spirit world free of any religious denomination,
going simply through the power of good will.

Above all, anthroposophy should help us in this task. It will lead us into the spirit land described, like a remote fairyland, in ancient Tibetan writings; the "land of Shambhala" means spirit world. We should enter this land, not in a trance, but in full consciousness and guided by Christ. Even now, initiates must go often to the land of Shambhala, so that they can draw new forces from there. Later, other human beings, too, will enter the land of Shambhala. People will see its radiant light, just as Paul saw the light above him, flowing from Christ. This light will stream toward them, also. The portals of this realm of light will open, and human beings will enter the holy land of Shambhala through them.

7 · The Return of Christ

Polermo, April 18, 1910

We are meeting here for the first time today, so let us speak about some intimate concerns of our spiritual science. To begin with, we will discuss the evolution of the human individuality in fairly general terms and next time in detail. We can understand the life of a single individual only when we also know the epoch in which that person lives. The human soul evolves through the ages, progressing from one incarnation to another. The soul's faculties today are not like they were during earlier periods. Today, they have reached the point where human beings can perceive the world of the senses and are able think through those perceptions inwardly. Before our time, it was completely different, because human souls still possessed a certain "dreamy" clairvoyance.

At that time, a person would not have been able to develop self-awareness, or I consciousness. Ancient, dreamlike clairvoyance had to disappear so that people would be limited to the sensory world and, through of a growing capacity for discernment of phenomenal appearances, gain self-awareness. In the future, we will win back the clairvoyance people once had and, at the same time, retain our sense of self-awareness.

This evolution has been gradual and continuous. Nevertheless, we can indicate the exact beginning of conscious, physical, sensory perception: 3101 B.C. Until then, a natural clairvoyance existed, then it gradually began to disappear, and the dark age called the lesser Kali Yuga began, and the human soul lost the ability to perceive the spirit world.

Now imagine the condition of human souls at the beginning of that dark age. When remembering past epochs, a human soul might say, "I once could see spirit beings; I could see into at least part of the world where the ancient Rishis and Zarathustra were teachers, and I could listen to those great leaders and masters of ancient times.[1] I could hear great leaders speak to me of wisdom from the spirit world." This feeling, however, grew continually weaker in those souls.

Three thousand years after the beginning of that dark age, a new possibility arose for human beings to unite with the spirit world. This possibility arose from the fact that one could unite with the spirit world through one's I-being; in other words, it was possible to perceive the spirit world even though human perception was limited to the senses. This possibility arose through the incarnation of Christ. The other great world leaders incarnated in such a way that their spiritual being united with an astral body. When we try to understand the essence of the Bodhisattvas, we find that their spirit portion, which worked on earth, ascended to higher worlds linked only to the astral body. We find that Christ is the only divine spirit being with a direct connection to a physical body. This means that

---

1. The ancient Iranian name Zarathustra (or Zoroaster, as the Greeks called him) cannot be ascribed any precise historical individual or time. Academic opinion, based on linguistic analysis of the oldest texts, suggests a date around 1500 B.C., whereas Greek sources suggest dates as diverse as 6000 to 500 B.C.

the I-being of Jesus abandoned his physical, ether, and astral sheaths, and the Christ incarnated as the I within those sheaths. Thus, every human I-being can have a connection with the Christ. In earlier ages, the great leaders of humanity could be perceived in such a way that people could understand their bond with the spiritual world only through images. Now, by contrast, the whole life story of Christ consists of facts that could be expressed in the physical world. In other words, the Christ event can be comprehended through our intellect, using our physical mind. God had to descend to the physical world, because the human faculty for perception could no longer rise above the world of physical senses. Thus arose the powerful prophecy of John the Baptist, that the soul's disposition must be changed so that the kingdom of heaven can draw near.

In earlier times, one could approach the kingdom of heaven, to some degree, through human clairvoyance. Now one would have to find it in Christ through the human senses. Christ descended to the physical plane so that humanity would not lose its connection with the spirit world during Kali Yuga. This dark age lasted more than five thousand years. We now live in the important time at the end of Kali Yuga, which began in 3101 B.C. and ended in 1899. Since then, certain soul faculties have slowly begun to develop, though are not yet recognized by human science. During the twentieth century, new human soul faculties will gradually evolve in some people. Before the end of the century it will be possible, for example, to perceive the human ether body. Another faculty will allow one to look within and see, as though in a dream, an image of a future act. Some will be endowed in such a way that they will have yet another experience; Paul's personal experience near Damascus will become common for certain people.

We can understand the significance of this twentieth-century event when we consider this: Paul heard about everything that happened in Palestine, but it could not change him from Saul to Paul. Because of his soul disposition, he remained unconvinced that the man from Nazareth was indeed the Christ. Through clairvoyant awareness of the event near Damascus, however, he was able to say for the first time that the Christ exists. Those who will experience the event of Damascus during the twentieth century will receive direct knowledge of the Christ. They will not need documentation to know of Christ; they will have direct knowledge, which is possessed only by initiates today. All the faculties that can now be gained through initiation will be universal human faculties in the future. Esoterically, this soul condition is called "the second coming of Christ." Christ will not incarnate again physically; he will appear in an ether body, as he did on the road near Damascus.

Christ incarnated on the physical plane when humanity had become limited to the physical body. We can repeat today the words of John the Baptist, "Repent...for the kingdom of heaven is at hand." In other words, change the disposition of your soul so that your faculties open to the spirit world. Those with etheric clairvoyance will thus see the Christ appear to them in an ether body. The faculties I have described are like seeds in the soul. In the future they will be developed, and we must say that human destiny will lie, to a certain extent, in one's own hands.

Once etheric vision does appear, however, people will have to recognize its significance. Such people will not be able to fall back on materialistic views, as is done today. This faculty will not be immediately obvious, and those who have it may even be considered sick or deluded. It is therefore the mission of spiritual science to prepare people to understand this. Communicating the basic ideal of spiritual science thus is not an option but necessary for human evolution.

What we have said will often be repeated in the years to come, but it is vital that this be understood correctly. It is possible that materialistic tendencies will penetrate the Theosophical Society, even to the point that people will believe that the Christ will assume a material body when he returns.[2] If Christ were to do this, one could say that humanity has not progressed at all during the last two millennia. Christ appeared two thousand years ago in a physical body and was perceived by the physical senses. For future clairvoyance he will appear in an ether body.

Through spiritual science, we are preparing ourselves to understand the significant era ahead. To be anthroposophists, it is not enough to approach spiritual science as a theory; it must be brought to life within us. This great event must be observed with complete precision. Because of the materialistic direction of theosophy today, some ambitious people will try to profit by creating the belief that they are the Christ, and there will be those who believe them. For true anthroposophists, this will be a test, and they will have to arm themselves against such attempts by elevating human feeling into the spirit worlds instead of debasing them in this way. Those who understand anthroposophy correctly will be able to say to the false messiahs

2. A short time later, the Theosophical Society in Adyar proclaimed the rebirth of the Christ in an Indian boy named Jiddu Krishnamurti (1895–1986), who later rejected that claim. Steiner objected, and his dissent led to the exclusion of the German Section of the society, of which Steiner was the General Secretary. See Rudolf Steiner, *From the History & Contents of the First Section of the Esoteric School, 1904–1914,* (Anthroposophic Press, 1998; GA 264), part 2.

of the twentieth century: You have announced the appearance of Christ in the physical world, but we know that Christ will manifest only in an etheric form. True anthroposophists will wait for Christ's appearance to the higher senses. People must understand, before death, the real meaning of Christ's second coming; then, in the life between death and rebirth, this understanding will open the spiritual senses. Those who do not have these faculties and have been unable to understand, while on earth, the significance of Christ's second coming must wait for another incarnation to acquire this understanding.

We now live in an extremely important era. We must describe Christ's second coming, which will be perceived by clairvoyants. We can describe this event by looking at the cosmos and an approaching event—the appearance of Halley's Comet, an important area of study for Rosicrucian theosophists. Its appearance is related to events in the spirit world. The movements of planets around the sun corresponds to normal events in human evolution; the appearance of a comet corresponds to an influence that counters normal events. Rosicrucian research demonstrates that every comet exerts a particular influence on human evolution.[3] The particular influence of Halley's Comet has to do with an intense push toward materialism. Every time this comet has appeared, there has been a renewed movement toward materialism. Its appearance in 1759 corresponded with the time when Voltaire's ideas reached their peak. Its appearance in 1835 corresponded with the materialism of Moleschott, Büchner, and others.[4] Likewise,

---

3. *Rosicrucian,* as used here, is not connected directly with the Theosophical Society. Steiner refers to a modern path of spiritual investigation, not to be confused with various groups that claim to be Rosicrucians.
4. See footnote on page 68.

in our time there will be a new impulse toward materialism, an outer sign of which is the appearance of Halley's Comet. Those who allow themselves to be swayed by its influence will fall into deep materialism.

Today, we have not only this impulse but also an influence that will lift humanity to the spirit heights. Those who understand the signs of the times will understand this. In the macrocosm, the indication of this is that the sun, at the vernal equinox, has entered the sign of Pisces, the Fish. When Christ appeared, the sun was in the sign of Aries, the Ram. The sun entered this sign around 800 B.C. and was well into Aries by the time of the event of Golgotha. The sun has been in the sign of Pisces for several centuries. In the near future, it will have advanced so far in this sign that it will become the visible symbol for the reappearance of Christ in an etheric body. You will see, therefore, that the teachings of anthroposophy do not arise from mere theories; rather, the task of our teaching is provided by the signs of the times. This message has been foreseen in the West for many centuries by those who call themselves Rosicrucians. Their teachings include a fifth gospel, along with the four that are better known.[5] These other four can be understood through this fifth gospel, which will be given to some during the twentieth century, just as the others were given around the time of the physical appearance of Christ. Rosicrucians who have a clear consciousness will understand the significance this fifth gospel has for humanity.

If you will become attentive to Rosicrucian theosophy, your efforts will be able to join the spirit of human progress, and it will become possible for you to understand the Christ who will

---

5. See footnote on page 30.

appear in a new form. The time is at hand when we will be able to recognize the Christ directly, even if all records of the Gospels were to be lost.

One can speak of these things only with a group that has been thoroughly prepared by theoretical learning, but also by continually breathing the very air of our group life. In public lectures one must observe certain limits, but in this group we breathe air in which these great truths can be discussed. Our souls, however, should not be satisfied by merely speaking about such truths; we should also gain strength for daily work—a light that will stream into ordinary daily life—and strength for the future. We must become wise through truth, but we must also continue to speak courageously of the truth, as though it were spiritual blood that we let flow into our feeling and will.

8 · The Etheric Vision of the Future

Hanover, May 10, 1910

People often ask why the teachings of spiritual science must be given now, whereas a hundred and twenty years ago, for example, no one heard anything about it. In fact, spiritual truths have always been communicated, though in a different form from today. During the seventeenth and eighteenth centuries, the teachings came from small brotherhoods, and, for good reasons, they were written down not by the originators but by others. Only scanty accounts penetrated out of those early mystery schools. Even today, one can find one or two books in whose dim pages (dim only on the surface) are quite wonderful. Such a book, *Aurea Catena Homeri*, was mentioned by Goethe.[1] What its pages reveal will seem like fantastic nonsense to modern readers, especially the most "enlightened" ones. If one approaches this so-called nonsense with the tools of spiritual science, however, one finds something very different. The greatest secrets are disclosed to one who carefully studies its pages. In earlier times, only a few could advance to this esoteric

---

1. Anton Joseph Kirchweger, *Aurea Catena Homeri* ("The Golden Chain of Homer," 1723), a book on alchemical illustrations.

science, but now there are unlimited opportunities for anyone with a heartfelt longing to go there. How has this come about, and why may these secrets now be revealed to the public?

There is almost no historical age that cannot be described as a time of transition. Every age is said to be so, more or less, with justification. In our time, fundamental events are happening, and it may be called correctly an era of transition. To understand the deep bases of our age, we must consider some well-known facts. We are approaching an era when one must ascend to higher worlds with clear, clairvoyant consciousness. The old Atlantean clairvoyance ended around 3101 B.C., and people began to perceive their environment with an understanding bound to the brain. Clairvoyant consciousness had to be darkened in humankind for a certain time so that human beings could fully master the physical world. The lesser Kali Yuga began and lasted five thousand years; it ended in 1899.

Now the time is being prepared when it will become possible for people to develop delicate clairvoyant faculties, even without special training. From 1930 to 1950, some will see something like a bright band of light around certain people. Others will see something like a strange dream arising. Perhaps one has just finished doing something, and an image might appear in the soul to show what action must eventually be taken to compensate for that action. If a person with these faculties speaks of such experiences, the response might be, "There have always been those who understand what you have seen. They call it the 'human ether body,' and it is karma that arises in you like a dream."

This age is one of etheric clairvoyance; it will redeem the previous age in which thinking and understanding were bound to the brain. Spiritual science is needed so that this time will not go by unnoticed. The Christ needed a forerunner, and, similarly, spiritual science had to appear to prepare for the age of clairvoyance. Something could certainly happen now that would crush the bud of these delicate soul faculties; this danger exists when people will not listen to the teachings of spiritual science. Those with these faculties would then be called fools and be put away in mental hospitals. Many will even believe that they themselves have been hallucinating; others will be afraid to speak of them, dreading the ridicule. All this can lead to the destruction of these new faculties of soul. Clever and "enlightened" persons in that era will then say, "Forget about it. People long ago declared that our age would see individuals with special soul faculties. Where are they? We are not aware of them." Nevertheless, the prophecy of spiritual science will have been fulfilled. Although everything might be stifled by the increasing power of materialism, today we can expect from an understanding for the freer and lighter age just beginning.

Everything that happens in the world affects everything else, and the microcosm corresponds to the macrocosm. Let us study world events as they relate to us. People are easily satis- fied by asserting the truth of something, but spiritual science is not really concerned with emphasizing the truth of something so much as the fact that something is important. For example, much is said and written about the similarity between human and animal skeletons. This is certainly a fact that one would not argue about; yet there are facts that are much more impor- tant. There is a fact everyone can observe right before our eyes, and yet it is connected with a great cosmic event. This is the truth that the human is the only being who walks erect. It is often said that the human skeleton and that of the ape are sim- ilar, but that the upright walk of the ape was botched. The ape tried to walk upright but failed. The ability of human beings to walk upright is connected with the sun and the earth and their spiritual effects on each other. The sun and earth had to separate from each other before humankind could walk erect. Animals are earthbound, but human beings have raised themselves, and our view is thus turned upward. We walk in a vertical position, and our erect gait is a continuation of the earth's radius. We must begin to feel the importance of this truth.

Let us consider another important instance of correspondence between macrocosm and microcosm. In outer form, one is male or one is female. It is important to consider, however, that this is true only of the outer form, not of one's inner being (we are speaking now of the outer characteristics in one incarnation). What polarity in the macrocosm corresponds to this appearance of masculine and feminine? We can clarify this by looking into cosmic space. There we find substances that have remained behind—they have not taken up the laws of the sun and earth but remained at the ancient moon stage of evolution. Just the opposite is true of the present moon, which has gone through its own evolution. Because of this, it become too hardened. It had to dry out and freeze, because it went past its normal development. It is a future Jupiter condition that has gone awry, like a small boy with the constitution of an old man. The moon thus missed its strength by going too far, leading to its own death.

Typically, people will swear by a truth that they received as an abstract principle; but in concrete terms, this same truth appears to be an illusion. In theosophical books one always finds the remark that the world is an illusion, or maya. Every theosophist "knows" this as a fact and often repeats it. To say that a male or female body is merely an illusion contributes something concrete to the abstraction. It is a fact that neither the masculine nor the feminine body is properly developed (except for the head). The female body is not fully developed, whereas the male body has gone too far in its development. There is no middle ground here. The feminine form is unreal because it is not fully developed; the masculine form went too far beyond the middle ground of development. Great artists have always sensed these imperfections. Clothing arose from an intense feeling for this fact. Ancient priestly robes were supposed to represent the ideal of the human body. Only sensual people can devote themselves to nudist colonies, because they cannot recognize a higher expression of the body they see.

Consequently, the lunar body has gone too far in evolution, and there are bodies such as comets that have remained at an early stage of evolution. You may wonder what all this has to do with men and women. A comet brings the laws of the earlier moon and thus renews these ancient laws. It also brings cyanide compounds, which has been known for a long time to esoteric science and was recently established by physical science. Just as oxygen and carbon compounds are necessary to us on earth, so the cyanides were essential on the ancient moon. At the 1906 annual meeting of the Theosophical Society in Paris, I enlarged on this matter in the presence of Colonel Olcott (our president at the time) and various others.

Because a woman's body has remained behind in its development, it has preserved a softer, more flexible, less substantial materiality; her brain can be ruled more easily by spirit. A man, however, having rushed ahead in his development, now has difficulty overcoming his rigid material and more impermeable brain substance. For this reason, a woman is more receptive to new ideas; her soul takes possession of them, and she can more easily direct her thoughts through the brain. It is harder for a man to mobilize the rigid parts of his brain. So it's logical that, for example, there are more women than men in the Theosophical Society, a fact that various individuals deplore. Perhaps men who dread the thought of appearing as women in a later incarnation will find these facts somewhat consoling.

Let us now apply the law of correspondence between macrocosm and microcosm to another important matter. In ordinary life we sometimes experience humdrum days; we wake up, go to bed, wake up again, and just do our jobs. It is also this way in the far reaches of space. Everything takes its usual course; the sun rises and sets again and again, in a regular rhythm. And, just as a family's routine is interrupted when a child is born and a completely new impulse enters earthly existence with this spiritual being, likewise the appearance of a new heavenly body such as a comet has a similar effect in space.

All matter is the expression of spirit, and esoteric science is able to say what lies behind the phenomena. The way modern science tries to study comets is like a fly trying to observe the Sistine Madonna. As it crawls over the painting, it sees the colors—a spot of red here, a little blue there—but beyond this it sees nothing at all. This sort of "fly science" knows nothing of those inner principles, whose outer sign is the comet. Halley's Comet in particular tends to drive humanity further into materialism. Without this comet, the books of the Encyclopedists would not have appeared, and there would have been no articles from Moleschott and Büchner after 1835.[2] Today the ominous sign of this comet is appearing again, and spirituality will

---

2. Encyclopedists were the writers of a French encyclopedia (1751–1780). They were identified with the Enlightenment and advocated deism and scientific rationalism. See also the footnote on page 68.

receive a death blow unless people listen to what spiritual science has to say and put it to use.

There is another significant sign, however, whose forces are stronger than those of the comet; it offers humanity the possibility of escape from the comet's destructive influence. This is the spring sign of Pisces, the Fish, through which we have been passing for several centuries. At the time of Christ, the vernal equinox was in the constellation of Aries, the Ram. We are thus well into this sign of great spiritual forces, which will carry us upward. By understanding these forces, we can develop the faculties available in this sign.

Humankind rises to true human dignity only through a deep understanding of the fundamental relationships of the spirit. People should not rush blindly past what cosmic signs have to show us. Wisdom should enlighten the association between microcosm and macrocosm. Take, for example, the wisdom contained in an ant hill's structure. It has meaning as a whole, and every ant experiences itself as a member of a whole. Human society, however, is regulated according to what its members consider useful to themselves as individuals. People run past one another without any sense or understanding. Human life is really foolish in many ways.

Those who take up an inner discipline, however, ripen themselves for what should be stated as the third fact: the possibility of seeing into the etheric world with newly awakened faculties. There the soul will see what Paul saw: the Christ in his ether body. For those who have made themselves worthy of it, this great event—the second coming of Christ—will take place with no need of books or documents. It is anthroposophy's task to announce this. There are people now who sense the fact that we have overcome the Dark Age and that we are approaching a more luminous time. Anthroposophists must walk this path consciously. Spiritual science must bring its fruits to humankind, so that souls become capable of joining with Christ. It makes no difference whether those souls inhabit a physical body or not; Christ descended to those who have died as well as to those who are alive on earth. The great, sublime event of Christ's appearance in the ether is significant for all.

9 · The Etherization of the Blood

Basel, October 1, 1911

As human beings, whenever we work toward knowledge—whether as mystics, realists, or in any other way—we have been commanded to know ourselves. Nevertheless, it has been repeatedly emphasized on other occasions, that knowledge of the human soul is certainly not as easy to acquire as people often believe, even anthroposophists. Anthroposophists should always be mindful of the hindrances we encounter in our efforts. Self-knowledge is absolutely essential, however, if we wish to attain a worthwhile goal in world existence, and if our actions are to be worthy of us as members of humankind. Let us ask why self-knowledge is so difficult for us. Human beings are truly complicated, and when we speak of the inner life of our souls, we should not assume that it is a simple matter. We need patience and perseverance and the will to penetrate continually more deeply into this wonderful organization of divine spirit forces that manifest as a human being.

Before we look into the nature of self-knowledge, two aspects of human soul life present themselves to us. Just as a magnet has a north and a south pole, and just as light and darkness present themselves as two poles of light, there are also two poles in our soul life. Both poles may appear as we observe someone involved in two contrasting life situations. Imagine we are watching a woman standing on the street, and she is completely lost in contemplating the striking beauty and wonder of some natural phenomenon. We see how still she stands, moving neither her hands nor her feet, never looking away from the spectacle presented to her. We are also aware that she is making an inner picture of what she sees. We say that she is absorbed in contemplation of what surrounds her. That is one situation; here is another. A man is walking along the street and senses that someone has insulted him. Without really thinking about it, he becomes angry and hits the one who insulted him. Here we see a manifestation of the forces that spring from anger—impulses of will—and it's easy to imagine that, if the action had been preceded by thought, there would have been no need to strike.

We have imagined two very different actions. In the first, there is only the formation of a mental picture, a process free of conscious will; in the second, there is no thought, no formation of mental pictures, and a will impulse is given immediate expression. These two situations present us with the two poles of the human soul. One is surrender to contemplation and to forming mental pictures and thought, in which volition does not take part; the second is an impelling force of will without thought. We arrived at these facts simply by outer observation of ordinary life.

We can go into these things more deeply, however, and enter areas where we find our way only by calling on the results of esoteric research to help us. Here, another polarity confronts us: sleeping and waking. We know the esoteric significance of the relationship between sleeping and waking. Elementary concepts of anthroposophy tell us that, when we are awake, the four members of our being (physical body, ether body, astral body, and I-being) are organically and actively interwoven; but while in sleep, the physical and ether bodies remain together in bed as the astral body and I-being pour out into the great cosmos that border on our physical existence. We could also approach these facts from a different direction. What can be said about waking life—contemplation of the world, imagination, thinking, and will impulses—on the one hand, and sleep, on the other.

You can see that, if we penetrate this question more deeply, it becomes obvious that, in our present physical existence, people are essentially always asleep, in a certain sense. At night people sleep in a different way than they do in the daytime. This can be proved to you in a purely external way, since you know that one can awaken in the esoteric sense during the day—that is, one can attain clairvoyance and see into the spirit world. The ordinary physical body is asleep to this observation, and one can rightly say that when a person learns to use the spiritual senses, it is an awakening. At night, of course, we are asleep in the ordinary way. We can say, therefore, that while asleep in the ordinary sense, people "sleep in the physical world," and today's daytime consciousness is "sleep in the spirit world."

If people are unaware that volition is not asleep during the night, this is because they understand only how to be awake in their thinking. But the will does not sleep during the night; it works within a fiery element upon one's body to restore what was used up during the day. These facts can be considered in yet another light. On deeper scrutiny, we see that, in the ordinary waking condition of physical life, as a rule, people have little control over the will; volition detaches itself from daily life. Observe closely what we call the human will, and you will see how little control people have over the will in daily life. Just consider everything you do from morning until evening, and how little of it is really the result of your own thinking, imagination, or individual decisions. When someone knocks at the door and you say "Come in," this really cannot be called a decision of your thinking and volition. If you are hungry and sit down to a meal, this cannot be called a decision of the will, because it is really the result of your organism's needs. Try to picture your daily life, and you will see how little it is directly influenced by your will.

Why is this? Esoteric teachings show us that, in terms of the will, people in fact sleep during the day; in other words, people do not really live within their will impulses. We can invent better concepts, and we can become increasingly moral and refined as individuals, but we can do nothing about the will. If we cultivate better thoughts, we can indirectly affect the will, but we cannot directly influence the will in life. This is because, in our daily life, our will can be influenced only indirectly—through sleep. While asleep, you do not think; you do not form mental images, but the will awakes and permeates our organism from outside and invigorates it. We feel strengthened in the morning, because the will has penetrated our organism. The fact that we do not perceive this will activity and know nothing about it becomes comprehensible when we realize that all conceptual activity sleeps whenever we sleep.

To begin with, then, we will offer this suggestion for further contemplation and meditation. You will see that, as you progress in self-knowledge, you will find confirmation of the truth that people sleep in their will while awake and sleep in their conceptual life while asleep. The life of will sleeps by day; the life of thought sleeps by night.

Thus there are two poles in human beings: that of observing and forming mental images and that of will impulses. Human beings are related in entirely opposite ways to these two poles, but these are the extremes; soul life as a whole exists in various nuances between these two poles, and we can begin to understand this soul if we view it as a microcosm and compare it to what we know as the higher worlds.

From what has been said, we know that the process of mental imagery is one pole of soul life. This process seems unreal to those whose thinking is materialistic. We often hear the notion that mental pictures and thoughts are only mental pictures and thoughts. This implies that, when we handle a piece of bread or meat, this is a reality, but a thought is "only a thought." This means that you cannot eat a thought, and thus a thought is not real but merely a thought. But why is this? Essentially, it is because what people consider thoughts may be compared to what thoughts really are, just as we can compare the reflected image the thing in itself. The reflected image of a flower points you to the flower in its reality. So it is with thoughts: human thinking is a shadow of mental images and beings that belong to a higher world called the astral plane.

A correct representation of thinking would be to picture the human head as in this drawing (it is not absolutely correct but simply a schematic sketch). There are thoughts in this head, represented by dashes. These thoughts in the head, however, must be imagined as beings that live on the astral plane. Beings that vary widely are active as abounding mental images and activities that cast their shadow images into human beings; these processes are reflected in the human head as thinking.

Continuous streams flow from your head into the astral plane, and these shadows establish thought life in your head.

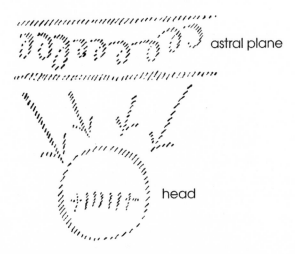

In addition to what we call thinking, there is another process in the human soul. Ordinarily, one distinguishes between thinking and feeling (this is not strictly correct, but it is useful to take a concept from ordinary life). Feelings fall into two categories: feelings of pleasure and sympathy and feelings of displeasure and antipathy. The first are stimulated by good, benevolent actions and the second by evil, malevolent actions. This is different and involves more than the just forming of mental images. We mentally form images of things regardless of other factors. The soul, on the other hand, experiences sympathy or antipathy in relation to beauty and goodness or ugliness and evil. Everything that takes place as human thinking indicates the astral plane; everything connected with sympathy or antipathy points to the realm we call the lower devachan. I drew lines to indicate the connection between mental images and the astral world, and now I can show that feeling point upward to devachan, or the heavenly world. Processes in the heavenly world, or devachan, are projected mainly into our breast as feelings of sympathy or antipathy toward beauty or ugliness and for good or evil. Within our souls, there are shades of the heavenly world, or lower devachan, in what we may call our experience of the moral and esthetic world.[1]

There is also a third aspect of the human soul, which we must distinguish strictly from a simple preference for beneficial actions. There is a difference between standing by and taking pleasure in seeing a kind act and activating one's volition to perform such an act oneself. The pleasure one takes in seeing good and beautiful acts or the displeasure one feels toward evil and ugly deeds I will call the esthetic element. The moral element, on the other hand, motivates one to do good. The moral element is at a higher level than the purely esthetic; mere pleasure or displeasure is at a lower level than the will to do something good or evil. Insofar as one's soul feels the need to express moral impulses, those impulses are the shadow images of higher devachan, of the higher heavenly world.

We can easily imagine these three stages of soul activity: purely intellectual (thoughts, mental pictures, observation); esthetic (pleasure or displeasure); and moral (impulses to do good or evil). These are microcosmic reflections in human experience of the three realms that exist in the macrocosm at ascending levels. The astral world is reflected in the world of thought and intellect; the lower devachan is reflected in the

1. Devachan (Tibetan), literally "the happy place." Steiner also uses other terms to describe areas of the soul: the region of soul life = upper devachan; the region of active soul power = lower devachan; the region of soul light = astral. See Rudolf Steiner, *Theosophy*, pp. 103–108.

esthetic realm of pleasure and displeasure; the higher devachan
world is reflected as morality.

Thoughts:	shadow images of beings of the astral plane	awake
Sympathy and antipathy:	shadow images of beings of the lower devachan	dreaming
Moral impulses:	shadow images of beings of the higher devachan	asleep

If we connect this with what was said about the polarity of
the human soul, we experience the intellect as the pole that
dominates the life in which we are intellectually awake. During
the day, people are awake to the intellect; while asleep, we are
awake to our will. Because we are asleep to our intellect at night,
we are unaware of what we do with the will. What we call moral
principles and impulses act indirectly in the will. Indeed, we
need sleep so that the moral impulses we absorb through thinking can become effective activity. In ordinary life today, people
are able to do what is right only at the level of intellect; they are
less capable of doing anything on the moral plane, because,
there, people depend on help from the macrocosm.

Inherent human nature can bring about the further development of the intellect, but we need the gods to help us acquire
greater moral strength. We sink into sleep so that we can
plunge into divine will, where the intellect does not interfere
and divine forces are transformed into the volitional strength
and moral principles we receive, instilling in our will something we could otherwise receive only into our thoughts.

Between these two opposites—the will that awakes at night
and the intellect that awakes by day—exists the sphere of

esthetic appreciation, which is always present in human beings. During the day, people are not fully awake; only the most unimaginative and pedantic individuals are always fully awake during the day. Basically, human beings must in fact dream during the day; they must be able to surrender to art or poetry or some other activity that is completely unconcerned with crass reality. Those who can surrender in this way create a bond that can enliven and invigorate the whole of existence. To give oneself up to such thoughts is, in a sense, like a dream penetrating waking life. You know that dreams enter sleep; these are real dreams that permeate the other consciousness of sleep. People also need this by day, otherwise they will lead a dry, empty, and unhealthy daily life. Dreams arise during sleep at night, in any case; this does not require proof. Midway between the two opposites of night dreaming and daydreaming there is a condition that can come alive in fantasy.

So, again, there is a threefold life of soul. The intellectual element in which we are really awake brings shadow images of the astral plane. This happens when, during the day, we give ourselves up to a thought, whereby fruitful ideas may originate for daily life and great inventions. Then, during sleep, we dream and our dreams play into our life of sleep, and images from lower devachan are reflected in us. When we work during sleep to impress morality upon our will, when we are able to imbue our thinking during the night with the influence of divine spiritual powers, the impulses we perceive are reflections from higher devachan. (We cannot perceive this directly, but certainly its effects.) These are the moral impulses and feelings that live in us. It leads us to say that, essentially, human life is justified only when we place our thoughts at the service of goodness and beauty and allow the heart's blood of divine spirit to flow through our intellectual activities, permeating them with moral impulses.

What we present here as the life of the human soul—first from exoteric observation and then from a more mystical kind of observation—is revealed by deeper esoteric research. The processes described in their outer qualities can also be perceived in human beings through clairvoyance. When a person stands before us today in a waking state and we observe that individual with clairvoyant sight, certain rays of light can be seen streaming continuously from the heart to the head. To sketch this schematically, we draw the region of the heart here and show continuous streams from there to the brain and flowing around the organ known to anatomy as the pineal gland.

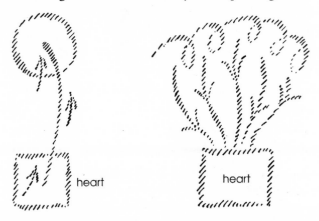

These rays of light flow from the heart to the head and around the pineal gland. These streams arise because human blood, a physical substance, continually dissolves into an etheric substance. In the region of the heart there is a continual transformation of the blood into this delicate etheric substance that streams upward toward the head and flows in a glimmering way around the pineal gland. This process is the etherization of the blood, and it can be shown in human beings throughout their waking life. However, this is different for human beings when asleep. When people sleep, the occult vision can see a continual stream into the brain from outside, and in the reverse direction as well, from the brain to the heart.

In sleeping people, streams come from outside—from the macrocosm of cosmic space—and flow into the inner constitution of the physical and ether bodies lying in bed. These streams reveal something remarkable when investigated; they vary greatly in different individuals. When asleep, people differ greatly from one another, and those who are a little vain would avoid going to sleep at public gatherings if they knew how much they betray themselves to esoteric observation. The streams that flow into human beings during sleep reveal distinct moral qualities through their particular colors; a person of lower moral principles reveals streams very different from those in a person of higher principles. Attempts to disguise one's nature during day are useless; in the face of higher cosmic powers, disguise is impossible. In cases of those who possess only a slight inclination toward moral principles, the rays flowing into them are brownish red or various shades tending toward brownish red. In those of high moral ideals, the rays are lilac to violet.

At the moment of awaking or going to sleep, a struggle, so to speak, occurs in the area of the pineal gland, between streams coming from above and streams rising from below. When people are awake, the intellectual element streams upward from below as currents of light, and the moral and esthetic nature flows downward from above. At the moment of waking or going to sleep, these two currents meet, and, in persons of low morality, a violent struggle takes place between the two streams in the area of the pineal gland. In those who possess a high morality and whose intellect flows outward, a glimmering light peacefully expands in the area of the pineal gland. This gland is almost surrounded by a small sea of light during the moments between awaking and sleeping. Moral nobility is revealed when a calm glow surrounds the pineal gland in those moments. Thus a person's moral character is reflected, and this calm glow of light often extends as far as the area of the heart. Two streams can thus be perceived in human beings: one from the macrocosm, the other from the microcosm.

To assess the full significance of how these two streams meet in the human being, we must first consider what has been said in a more external way about soul life and how this life reveals a threefold polarity of intellectual, esthetic, and moral elements that flow downward from above, from the brain toward the heart. We must also understand the full meaning of what was said about turning our attention to corresponding phenomenon in the macrocosm. As a result of the scrupulous, careful esoteric research of recent years by genuine Rosicrucians, these corresponding phenomenon can now be described.[2] Their investigations have shown that something takes place in the macrocosm that corresponds to what we've described in the microcosm. You will understand this better with time.

Right in the area of the human heart, blood is continually transformed into etheric substance, and a similar process takes place also in the macrocosm. We can understand this when we contemplate the Mystery of Golgotha and the moment when blood flowed from the wounds of Jesus Christ. This blood must not be thought of simply as a chemical substance, but because of all that has been said about the nature of Jesus of

---

2. See the footnote on page 111.

Nazareth, it must be recognized as something completely unique. When it flowed from his wounds into the earth, a substance was given to our earth that, by uniting with it, became the most important event for every age that followed on earth, and it could take place only one time. What happened to this blood in the ages that followed? The same thing that takes place in the human heart.

In earthly evolution, this blood has passed through a process of etherization. Just as our blood flows upward from the heart as ether, likewise, since the Mystery of Golgotha, the etherized blood of Jesus Christ has lived in the ether of the earth. The earth's ether body is imbued with what became of the blood that flowed on Golgotha. This is important; if that event through Jesus Christ had not taken place, the condition of humankind on the earth could not have been other than previously described. Since the Mystery of Golgotha, however, there has always been a possibility for the activity of the etheric blood of Christ to flow together with what streams in human beings from heart to head.

Because the etherized blood of Jesus is in the ether body of the earth, it accompanies the etherized human blood that flows upward from the heart to the brain; thus, not only do these streams I described earlier meet in the human being, but the human bloodstream also unites with the bloodstream of Jesus Christ. These two streams can unite, however, only if people are able to develop real understanding of the Christ impulse. Otherwise, there can be no union; the two streams will repel each other. In every age of earthly evolution, we must understand in a way that is appropriate for that time.

When Jesus Christ lived on earth, earlier events could be correctly understood by those who came to his forerunner John and were baptized by him according to the rite described in the Gospels. They were baptized so that their sin—the karma of previous lives that had come to an end—might be changed, and in order that they might realize that the most powerful impulse in earthly evolution was about to descend into a physical body. Human evolution progresses, however, and in our age it is important for people to understand that the knowledge of spiritual science must be received; that knowledge must be able to gradually kindle what streams from heart to brain, so that anthroposophy can be understood. If this happens, people will be able to comprehend the event that begins in the twentieth century: the appearance of the etheric Christ, as distinguished from the physical Christ of Palestine.

We have now reached the time when the etheric Christ enters the life of earth and will become visible—initially to a few people through natural clairvoyance, and then over the course of the next three millennia to more and more. This will inevitably happen as an event of nature. It will happen just as certainly as did the inventions related to electricity in the nineteenth century. Some will see the etheric Christ and will experience what took place near Damascus. This will not happen, however, until those people learn to observe the moment Christ approaches them. Only a few decades from now, a few people here and there will have certain experiences, particularly young people (this is already being prepared). And if they have truly sharpened their vision by working with anthroposophy, such individuals may become aware that someone has suddenly approached to help them become alert to something. The truth is, Christ has come to them, although they believe that they see a physical man. They will come to realize, however, that this is a suprasensory being, since he will immediately vanish. Many will have this experience while sitting silently in a room, oppressed with a heavy heart and not knowing which way to turn. The door will open, and the etheric Christ will appear to console that person. The Christ will become a living comforter. Though it may seem strange now, it is nevertheless true that even large numbers of people will often be sitting together and wondering what to do, and they will see the etheric Christ. He will be there and confer with them; he will cast his word into such gatherings. We are approaching those times, and this positive, constructive element will take hold of human evolution.

We will not say anything here against the tremendous progress in our culture today; these achievements are essential for human welfare and freedom. Whatever we gain in the way of external progress, however, by mastering the forces of nature is small and insignificant compared to the blessing upon those who experience a soul awakening through Christ, who will take hold of human culture and its concerns; unifying, positive forces will awaken in human beings. The Christ brings constructive forces into human civilization.

If we were to look back to early post-Atlantean times, we would find that human beings built their dwellings in a very different way that we do today. In those days, they used all sorts of growing things. Even when building palaces, they called on nature to help them by having plants and the branches of trees weave together and so on. Today, we must build with fragments. We make all external culture in our world with the products of fragmentation. During the coming years, you will gain an even better understanding of how much our culture is the product of destruction.

We thus realize what a tremendous advance was indicated by the fact that Christ needed to live for three years on earth in a specially prepared human body, so that he would be visible to physical eyes. Because of what happened during those three years, human beings have been prepared to see the Christ who will move among them in an ether body; he will enter earthly life as surely and effectively as did the physical Christ in Palestine. If human beings observe these events with undimmed senses, they will know that there is an etheric body that will move within the physical world, but they will know, too, that this is the *only* ether body that can work in the physical world as a human physical body does. It will differ from a physical body in this respect only: that it can be in two, three, or even a hundred or a thousand places at the same time. This is possible for an etheric but not a physical form.

The benefit to humanity provided by this advance is that the two poles I mentioned—the intellectual and the moral—will gradually come together and merge. This will occur because, over the next millennia, human beings will gradually learn to see the etheric Christ in the world; people will become imbued during waking life, too, through the effects of goodness directly from the spirit world. Presently, the will sleeps by day, and people can influence it only indirectly through thinking. However, from our time onward, something is at work in us under the aegis of Christ that, over the course of the next thousand years will make it possible for the activities of people while awake to have direct, beneficial effects.

Light is destroying itself in our post-Atlantean, earthly processes. Until the time of Atlantis, earthly processes had been progressive, but since then they have been processes of decay. What is light? Light decays, and decaying light is electricity. What we know as electricity is really light that is destroying itself within matter. The chemical force that is transformed in earthly evolution is magnetism. Yet a third force will become active, and if it seems electricity works wonders today, this third force will affect civilization in an even more miraculous way. The more of this force we employ, the faster the earth will tend toward becoming a corpse, while its spiritual part prepares for the Jupiter embodiment. Forces must be applied to destroy the earth so that human beings can be freed from it, and so that the earth's body can fall away. As long as the earth's processes were progressive, this was not happening, since only a decaying earth can use the great achievements of electricity. As strange as this sounds, it must gradually become known. We must understand the process of evolution before we can assess our culture in the right way. Thus we will learn that the earth has to be destroyed; otherwise, spirit will not be freed. We will also learn to value the positive penetration of spiritual forces into our earthly existence.

It was Socrates' dream that one day virtue could be taught; now, not only will it will become increasingly possible on earth to energize the human intellect through such teaching, but also for moral impulses to be spread abroad. Schopenhauer (1788–1860) suggested that to preach morality is easy, but to establish it is difficult. Why is this? Because morality has yet to be spread through preaching; it is, after all, possible to recognize moral principles and yet not live by them. For most people, the Pauline saying applies here: the spirit is willing but the flesh is weak. This will change through the moral fire that streams from the Christ. Because of this, it will become increasingly clear to people that the world needs moral impulses. Human beings will transform the earth as they increasingly feel that morality is essential to our world. In the future, immorality will be possible only for those who receive immoral help and are pushed in that direction—people who are possessed by evil demons, by ahrimanic and asuric forces and who work for such possession. The future of the earth will be such that, although there will be enough people who teach morality and offer a moral foundation, there will be those who by their own choice surrender to evil forces, thus enabling an excess of evil to struggle against the benevolent portion of humankind. Nobody will be forced to one choice or another; matters will proceed according to the free will of each individual.

Then a time will come when the earth enters conditions that, like much else, are described only by Eastern mysticism. The atmosphere of morality will have gathered considerable strength, which has been spoken of for many millennia by Eastern mysticism. Since the coming of Gautama Buddha, it has spoken especially about a future condition when earth will be bathed in a moral etheric atmosphere. Ever since the time of the ancient Rishis, Eastern mystics had hoped that this moral impulse would come to earth from Vishva Karman (or from Ahura Mazda, as Zarathustra proclaimed). Eastern mysticism foresaw that this moral atmosphere would come to earth from the being we call the Christ. Eastern mystics had set their hopes on the being of Christ.

Eastern mystics could imagine the consequences of that event but not its form. They imagined that, within five millennia after the Buddha's enlightenment, pure akashic forms bathed in fire and lit by the sun would appear in the wake of the one who could not be seen by the Eastern mysteries. In fact, this is a wonderful image: that something would come to prepare the way for the Sons of Fire and Light to move through the moral atmosphere of the earth—not in physical form but in pure akashic forms within the earth's moral atmosphere. It

was said that five thousand years after the Buddha's enlightenment, a teacher would be present to show humankind the
nature of those wonderful, pure forms of fire and light. That
teacher, Maitreya Buddha, will appear three millennia from
now and teach people about the Christ impulse.

Eastern mysticism thus joins Western Christian knowledge
to form a beautiful unity. It will also be revealed that the one
who will appear in three thousand years as Maitreya Buddha
will have incarnated repeatedly on the earth as a bodhisattva to
succeed Gautama Buddha. One of his incarnations was that of
Jeshu ben Pandira, who lived a hundred years before the beginning of our Christian era. The being who incarnated in Jeshu
ben Pandira is the one who will one day become Maitreya Buddha, one who returns repeatedly, century after century, in a
body of flesh, not yet as a buddha but as a bodhisattva. Even in
our time, the one who will be Maitreya Buddha gives the most
significant teachings concerning the Christ and the Sons of Fire
(Agnishvattas) of Indian mysticism.

True Eastern and Christian wisdom both provide the indications by which people can recognize the being who will be Maitreya Buddha. In contrast to the Sons of Fire, Maitreya Buddha
will appear in a physical body as a bodhisattva, and he can be
recognized by the fact that his development during youth shows
no indication of the individual within him. Only those who
understand will recognize the presence of a bodhisattva, who will
not manifest before the ages of thirty to thirty-three. Something
like an exchange of personality takes place at that time. Maitreya
Buddha will reveal his identity to humanity in the thirty-third
year of his life. Just as Jesus Christ began his lifework in his thir-
tieth year, so do bodhisattvas, who will continue to proclaim the
Christ impulses, reveal themselves in their thirty-third year.

The transformed bodhisattva, Maitreya Buddha, will speak in powerful words that cannot be adequately described at the present time; he will proclaim the great mysteries of existence. Maitreya Buddha will speak in a language that must first be created, because no human being today can find the words that Maitreya Buddha will use to address humankind. Human beings cannot yet be addressed in this way, because the physical instrument for this form of speech does not exist yet. The teaching of the Enlightened One will not flow into human beings as mere teachings; they will pour as moral impulses into human souls. Such words cannot be spoken today by the physical human larynx; in our time those words can be present only in spirit worlds.

Anthroposophy is a preparation for all that will come in the future. Those who are serious about the human evolutionary process will resolve not to let soul development come to a halt; they will ensure that soul development eventually enables the spirit of the earth to become free, leaving the grosser part to fall away like a corpse. Humankind could frustrate the whole process, but those who want evolution to succeed must begin to understand spirit through what we now call anthroposophy. The cultivation of anthroposophy is thus a duty; knowledge is something that we can actually experience and toward which we are responsible. We should experience an inner awareness of this responsibility and resolve, experiencing the mysteries of the world so that we are aroused to enter anthroposophy. Spiritual science must not merely satisfy our curiosity, however; it must become a necessary part of our lives. Only when this happens will we experience our lives as building stones in the great construction of human souls and that will embrace all humanity.

Anthroposophy thus reveals the truth of world phenomena as it will confront future human souls, whether in a physical body or in the life between death and rebirth. The coming upheaval will concern even those who have laid aside the physical body. People must come to understand the earth while in the physical body, otherwise such events will have no meaning for them between death and a new birth. It will make no difference for those who acquire some understanding of Christ now, while in the physical body, whether they have already passed through the portal of death when the moment comes to see Christ. But for those who refuse to understand the Christ, if they have passed through the portal of death before that moment arrives, another opportunity will not present itself until another incarnation, because such knowledge cannot be learned between death and a new birth. Once the foundation has been laid, however, it endures, and Christ becomes visible also during the period between death and rebirth. Anthroposophy is not merely something we learn for earthly life; it also has value after we have laid aside the physical body at the time of death.

This is what I wanted to give you today as an understanding of humanity and to give you a handle for answering a great number of questions. Self-knowledge is difficult, because the human being is so complex. The reason for such complexity is that we are connected with all the higher worlds and beings. We have within us mirror images of the great cosmos, and the members of our constitution—material, ether, astral, and I-being—are really realms of divine beings. Our fourfold being forms one world; the other is a higher world: the world of heaven. For divine spirits, the higher worlds are bodily members in higher divine spirit worlds.

Human beings are complex, because we are truly a mirror image of the spirit world. Realization of this should make us aware of our inherent worth. However, we know that, although we are images of the spirit world, we nevertheless fall far short of what we should be. From this, aside from realizing our worth as human beings, we gain the right attitude of modesty and humility toward the macrocosm and the gods.

* * *

Rudolf Steiner's answers to questions at the end of the lecture

Question: How should we understand St. Paul's words about speaking in tongues (I Cor. 12:28–30 and 14:5–6)?

Answer: In exceptional persons, it may happen that, in addition to the phenomenon of speech while awake, something usually present only in sleep consciousness flows into speech. St. Paul spoke of this, and Goethe also spoke of it in the same sense; he wrote two interesting treatises about this phenomenon.

Question: How will one understand the consoling words of Christ?

Answer: People will experience these words as though they arise in their own hearts. They can also be received by physically hearing them.

Question: How do chemical forces and substances relate to the spirit world?

Answer: In the world, there are a number of substances that can combine with or separate from one another. What we call chemical action is projected into the physical world from the world of devachan—the realm of the harmony of the spheres. When two substances unite according to their atomic weights, they reflect two tones of that harmony of the spheres. The chemical affinity between two substances in the physical world is like a reflection from the world of the harmony of the spheres. Numerical ratios in chemistry are really an expression of the numerical ratios of the harmony of the spheres, which has itself become silent through the densification of matter. If we were able to dilute material substance into an etheric substance and perceive the atomic numbers as its inner formative principle, one could hear the harmony of the spheres.

There is a physical world, an astral world, lower devachan, and higher devachan. If you push the body even lower than the physical realm, you arrive in the subphysical world, the lower astral world, the evil lower devachan, and the evil higher devachan. The evil astral world is the province of Ahriman, and the evil higher devachan is the province of the Asuras.

The subphysical world:

Evil astral world (electricity):	the province of Lucifer
Evil lower devachan (magnetism):	the province of Ahriman
Evil higher devachan (terrible forces):	the province of the Asuras

If you drive chemical action below the physical plane, into the evil devachan, magnetism arises. If you force light down into the subphysical (that is, a stage lower than the material world), electricity arises. If the harmony of the spheres is pushed farther, down into the province of the Asuras, an even more terrible force is generated, which it will not be possible to hide much longer. One must imagine this force as far more powerful than the most violent electrical discharge, and we can only hope that, before someone discovers this force and delivers it into the hands of humankind, people will have rid themselves of everything immoral within them.

Question: What is electricity?

Answer: Electricity is light in the subphysical state, where it is compressed to the greatest degree. An inner quality must also be ascribed to light: light is itself at every point. Warmth can extend into the three dimensions of space, but with light we must speak of a fourth dimension. Light can extend itself in a fourfold way; it has the quality of inwardness as a fourth dimension.

Question: What will happen to the earth's corpse?

Answer: Our present moon circling the earth is the residue of the ancient Moon evolution. Similarly, there will be a residue of the Earth evolution that will circle Jupiter. These residues will gradually dissolve into the universal ether. In the case of the Venus stage of evolution, there will be no residue. Initially, Venus will manifest as pure warmth, then it will become light, and then it will pass into the spirit world. The residue from the Earth stage will be like a corpse. Human beings must not accompany earth along this path, however, because they would thereby be exposed to terrible torment. There are many beings, however, who will accompany this corpse, since they will develop to a higher stage by that means.

10 · Spirit Beings and the Ground of the World – I

Dornach, November 18, 1917

You will recall the studies in which we tried to establish a relationship to the various premises and assertions of modem psychoanalysis.[1] It was important to me to clarify the concept of the "unconscious," to show that the way it is commonly used in psychoanalysis is essentially groundless. We must go beyond this concept—a purely negative concept—and say that psychoanalysis works with inadequate methods of cognition concerning a phenomenon that is especially challenging today. Because psychoanalysts wish to explore the soul and spirit and, as we observed, even pursue soul and spirit into the social life, we have to say that we disagree with this even more than we do with what academic science has to say about this matter.

The dangers related to this matter must be regarded with great concern, because analytical psychology tries to intervene in life through education, therapy, and, probably before long, society and politics. We must ask: What is it, essentially, that researchers today cannot and do not wish to discover. They

---

1. See Rudolf Steiner, *Freud, Jung, and Spiritual Psychology* (Anthroposophic Press, 2001), Nov. 10–11, 1917 (GA 178).

recognize and search for a soul beyond consciousness, but they cannot rise to cognition of the spirit itself. In no way can spirit be comprehended through the concept of the unconscious, because unconscious spirit is like a person without a head. I have pointed out that there are those who, under certain hysterical conditions, walk the streets and see others with only their bodies, not their heads. It is a specific form of illness, this inability to see another person's head. Among researchers today, there are some who believe they see the whole spirit. Since they see spirit as unconscious, however, they immediately demonstrate that they have, themselves, fallen into illusion—the illusion that there could be spirit without consciousness, as though we had crossed the threshold of consciousness, whether in the right way, as we always describe it in spiritual scientific research, or in a sick, abnormal way, as in those cases usually submitted to psychoanalysts.

When one crosses the threshold of consciousness, one enters a realm of spirit; whether one enters the subconscious or the superconscious, one always enters a spirit realm. This is a realm, however, where spirit is conscious in a particular way and developing some form of consciousness. Where there is spirit, there is consciousness. We only have to look for the conditions under which a particular consciousness exists. Through spiritual science, it is possible to recognize the type of consciousness of a spirit being.

A week ago, a certain case was presented here. It involved a woman who left a social gathering and ran out in front of some horses; she was then prevented from jumping into a river and carried back to the house from which she had fled. There she was brought together with the master of the house, because in some unclear, subconscious way, she was in love with this man.

In this case, it cannot be said that the spirit that pushed her was unconscious or that it had an unconscious soul quality, though it certainly did not belong to this lady's consciousness. Indeed, it is something very conscious. The consciousness of the demonic spirit that led the lady back to her unlawful lover is indeed much shrewder in its consciousness than the lady is in her own muddled consciousness.

When human beings in any way cross the threshold of consciousness, the spirits that become active and powerful are not unconscious. Such spirits become consciously active and powerful in their own right. The expression used by psychoanalysts, "unconscious spirit," makes no sense at all. Speaking merely from my own perspective, I could simply say that the whole illustrious company sitting here is in fact my unconscious, as long as it is unfamiliar to me. It makes just as much sense to describe as unconscious the spirit beings around us that take hold of the personality under certain conditions, as happened in the situation I described a week ago. They are subconscious; they are not actually grasped by the consciousness that lives immediately within us, but they are themselves fully conscious.

It is very important to understand this, especially for the task of spiritual science in our time. Basically, this is because knowledge of a spirit world on the other side of the threshold and true self-knowledge is not merely an achievement of spiritual science today but, in fact, ancient knowledge. In earlier times, this was known only through ancient, atavistic clairvoyance. Today, we gradually learn and come to know this through other methods. The knowledge of real spirits must be found beyond human consciousness. Spirits live under conditions that are different from those of humanity, but they exist in continuous relationship to human beings; they can take hold of a person in thinking, feeling, and volition. This knowledge has always existed. It was always considered the secret treasure of particular brotherhoods, who treated such knowledge as strictly esoteric within their circles. Why did they treat it in this way?

To enlarge on this matter would lead us away from our subject, but it should be said that individual brotherhoods were permeated with an earnest conviction that most of humanity was not mature enough for this knowledge. This was indeed largely the case. There were other brotherhoods, however, that are called "brotherhoods of the left," who tried to possess this knowledge, because, when taken possession of by a small group, it would give it power over those without such knowledge. There have always been those whose aim was to secure power for certain groups over others. This could be accomplished by assuming a particular kind of knowledge to be an esoteric possession, while using it in such a way that the power was expanded and used to control something quite different.

Today, especially, we must be very clear about these matters. As you know, since 1879 humanity has been living in a very special spiritual situation (I enlarged on this in the previous lectures). Since 1879, extraordinarily powerful spirits of darkness have been shifted from the spiritual world into the human realm, and people who cling to the mysteries related to this and keep them wrongfully within small groups could cause anything imaginable with those secrets. Today I will show you exactly how certain mysteries relate to current development and how they can be used in the wrong way. You must be careful, however, to consider coherently all that I will say today (mostly of a historic nature) with what I will add tomorrow.

You all know that for a long time attention within our anthroposophic movement has been focused on the fact that the twentieth century should bring about a special relationship to the Christ in human evolution. This relationship will come about in the twentieth century. Even during the first half, as you know, a certain phenomenon will begin. It was suggested in my first mystery drama, in which a great many people perceived Christ in the etheric as an actual being.[2] We know that we truly live in the age of materialism.

We also know that, since the mid-nineteenth century, materialism has reached its climax. In reality, however, polarities must converge. It is exactly this climax of materialism in human evolution that must converge with an intensification of human evolution that leads to the ability to truly see Christ in the ether. One can imagine that ill will and resistance will be aroused in some people just by hearing of this mystery of seeing Christ and the new relationship between humanity and the Christ. These people would be members of certain brotherhoods who had hoped to exploit the event of the appearance of the etheric Christ—people who wished to use it for their own purposes and never allow it to become general human knowledge. There are brotherhoods, and they always influence public opinion by allowing one thing or another to be publicized in ways least noticed by most people.

Certain occult brotherhoods are spreading the message that the age of materialism has just about run its course and has, in a certain sense, already passed. These poor, pitiable, "smart" people spread the doctrine in numerous assemblies, books, and societies that materialism has exhausted itself and that one can again grasp something of spirit. But they can offer nothing

---

2. Rudolf Steiner, *Four Mystery Dramas* (Rudolf Steiner Press, 1978), "The Portal of Initiation: A Rosicrucian Mystery."

more than the word *spirit* and single phrases. These people are more or less in the service of those with an interest in lying—saying that materialism has been, so to speak, "ruined by poor management." This is not true; on the contrary, materialistic thinking is growing. It will thrive most while people deceive themselves into thinking they are no longer materialists. Materialistic thinking is increasing and will continue to increase for about four or five centuries.

As we have frequently emphasized here, it is necessary to comprehend this with clear consciousness and know that it is true. Humanity will truly heal when we work so thoroughly in spiritual life that we know with certainty that the fifth post-Atlantean epoch exists to uproot materialism completely from human evolution in general. It will take a more spiritual being, however, to counteract materialism. I have spoken in previous lectures about what people of the fifth post-Atlantean period must learn to encounter—that is, a fully conscious struggle against the evil arising in human evolution. During the fourth post-Atlantean cultural epoch, the task was to struggle with birth and death; now we face a struggle against evil. Thus, it is important now to grasp spiritual teaching in full consciousness, not to cast sand into the eyes of our contemporaries and pretend that the devil of materialism does not exist; in fact, he will thrive. Those who deal with these matters in the wrong way are just as aware of Christ's appearance as I am, but they deal with this event in a different way.

To understand this, one must keep an eye on a certain matter. Now that humanity has reached this point in the post-Atlantean era, there is a phrase that many people expound with comfortable smugness, but it is completely incorrect. They say, "As long as we live here from birth to death, our only concern is to surrender ourselves to life. Later on, if we are going to enter a spirit world when we die, it will be revealed to us in good time and we can just wait. We might as well enjoy life now as if this material world is the only one; if there is a spirit world waiting for us after death, it will reveal itself." This attitude is just as smart as saying, "Just as surely as there is a God in heaven, I am an atheist." It is this level of intelligence, and a common attitude, that the nature of things will all be revealed after death; meanwhile, it is not necessary to worry about spiritual science.

This attitude has always been arguable, but in the post-Atlantean period in which we live, it is especially ominous, because evil powers have urged this with special force upon humankind. When human beings, during current conditions of evolution, pass through the portal of death, they take with them the conditions of consciousness that they have created for themselves between birth and death. Those today who have focused exclusively on materialistic ideas, concepts, and sensory impressions in the phenomenal world condemn themselves after death to live in an environment where only those concepts defined during physical life have any meaning. People who have absorbed spiritual ideas enter the spirit world legitimately, but those who have rejected spiritual ideas are forced to remain, in a sense, within earthly conditions until they have learned (and this may be a long time) to absorb enough spiritual concepts that they can be carried by those ideas into the spirit world. Whether we absorb spiritual concepts or reject them, therefore, determines our environment on the other side of the threshold. Many of those souls (and this must be said with compassion) who have rejected or were hindered from absorbing spiritual concepts here in life are still wandering the earth and, although dead, remain bound to the earthly sphere. Such a soul, when no longer separated from a soul environment by the physical body (which can no longer prevent the soul from acting destructively), becomes a source of disturbance in the earthly sphere.

Let us look at what I would like to describe as a more normal situation: souls today pass into the spiritual world after death—souls who wished to know nothing at all about spiritual concepts and experiences. They become sources of disturbance, because they are kept within the earthly sphere. Souls who have been completely permeated here on earth by a relationship to the spiritual world are the only ones who pass through the portal of death so that they are received in the right way by the spiritual world. They will be carried away from the earthly sphere so that they can "spin threads" to those remaining behind—threads that are continually spun. We must be clear about this: the spiritual threads that exist between the souls of the dead and those of us who are bound to them are not sundered by death; after death, they remain, perhaps even closer, than they were here on earth. What I have said must be accepted as a serious, important truth.

I am not the only one with this knowledge; others are also aware of this at present. There are many, however, who exploit this truth in a terrible way. There are misguided materialists today who believe that material life is the only one. But there are also initiates who are materialists, and who spread materialistic teaching through brotherhoods. Do not be misled into believing that such initiates merely have the foolish idea that there is no spirit—that human beings do not have souls that can live independently of the body. You can be sure that anyone who has received a genuine initiation into the spirit world would never surrender to the foolishness of believing only in matter. There are many, however, who have a certain interest in encouraging the spread of materialism and who make all sorts of arrangements so that many people believe only in materialism and are totally under its influence. There are brotherhoods that have as their leaders initiates who have exactly such an interest in cultivating materialism and seeing it spread. These materialists are well served by the constant claim that materialism has already been overcome, because it is possible to advance some causes by saying the opposite. The way this is handled is often very complicated.

What do these initiates want? They know very well that the human soul is pure spirit—a being fully independent of the physical body. Despite knowing this, they protect and cultivate materialistic thinking among humankind. These initiates want the greatest possible number of souls between birth and death to absorb only materialistic ideas. In this way, souls are prepared to remain in the earthly sphere. To a certain extent, they become locked into the earthly sphere. Imagine established brotherhoods that are clearly aware of these circumstances. Such brotherhoods prepare certain human souls so that they remain in the material realm. It is then quite possible for these brotherhoods to arrange for those souls, after death, to come into the power sphere of their brotherhood, enabling the brotherhood to gain tremendous strength. These initiates are not materialists because of a disbelief in spirit; they are not that foolish and are very aware of spirit. They induce souls to remain with matter, even after death, to be available for their own purposes. These brotherhoods thus produce a clientele of souls who remain within the earthly realm. These souls of the dead possess forces that can be directed in many ways to bring about a variety of effects, and through this one can manipulate special powers in relation to those who have not been initiated in these matters.

This is simply an arrangement of certain brotherhoods. In such a matter, you can see clearly only when you do not allow yourself to be deceived by darkness and confusion and believe that such brotherhoods either do not exist or are harmless. They are by certainly not harmless; indeed, they are extremely harmful. They say that humankind should sink more deeply into materialism. And in keeping with the thinking of such initiates, they say that, whereas people should know that spiritual forces certainly exist, they are merely certain forces of nature.

I would like to describe for you the ideal that such brotherhoods maintain. One must exert a little effort to understand the situation. Imagine, therefore, a harmless world of people who are led somewhat astray by today's prevailing materialistic concepts; they have strayed a bit from the old, established religious ideas. Imagine this harmless humanity. Perhaps we can picture it graphically.

We imagine, here, the realm of harmless humanity (larger circle). As I said, this humanity is not completely clear about the spiritual world; led astray by materialism, they are unsure about how to act toward the spirit world. They are especially unclear how to act in relation to those who have passed through the portal of death. Imagine the realm of such a brotherhood is here (small green circle). This brotherhood spreads the teachings of materialism; it is concerned that people think strictly materialistic thoughts. In this way, the brotherhood brings about the procreation of souls who remain trapped in the earthly sphere after death. They will become a spiritual clientele for the lodge (orange). This means that they have created dead people who will not leave the earthly sphere, but remain on earth. With the right preparations, they can be retained in the lodges. As a result, lodges have been created that contain the living as well as the dead, and the dead are related to earthly forces.

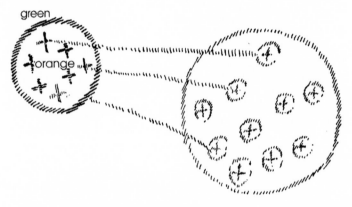

The matter is handled so that these people hold sessions just as people did in seances during the latter part of the nineteenth century, something I have spoken of often. It may then happen (and I ask you to keep this in mind) that events in those seances are directed by the lodge with the help of the dead. The true intention of the masters of those lodges, however, is to keep those people from knowing that they are dealing with the dead, but make them believe instead that they are dealing with higher forces of nature. People are made to believe that these are higher forces of nature—that psychism and similar phenomena are merely higher forces of nature. The true concept of soul will be taken from them, and it will be said that, just as there is electricity and magnetism, there are also higher forces. The fact that these forces are derived from human souls is hidden by the leaders in the lodge. Through this, however, those harmless souls gradually become completely dependent in their souls upon the lodge, without realizing what is subjugating them or the source of what is really directing them.

This is now beginning and will become more and more intense through the next five centuries. These evil brotherhoods are limiting themselves for now, but they are bound to continue their activity if they are not prevented, and they can be if one overcomes laziness toward the spiritual scientific worldview. The only remedy against this situation is knowledge of it. If you know about it, you are already protected. By understanding it to the extent that one's knowledge has become inner certainty, one is protected. You must not, however, be too lazy in your efforts to gain knowledge of these things. It must be said, however, that it is never really too late. I have often pointed out to you that these matters become clear only gradually, and I can only gradually pull together the elements that bring complete clarity.

I have often pointed out that, during the second half of the nineteenth century, many brotherhoods in the West introduced spiritism as an experiment. They did it as a test to convince themselves that they had gone far enough with humanity—to find out whether they had gone as far as they had intended. In their seances, they expected people to acknowledge the higher forces of nature. But these brothers of the left were disappointed that people said instead that spirits of the dead appear in the seances. That was a bitter disappointment to the initiates; it was exactly what they did not want, because it was this belief in the dead that those initiates wanted to take away from humanity. Not the activity of the forces of the dead, but the knowledge that those forces derive from the dead—this correct, significant thought—was to be taken from people. The brothers see this as a higher materialism; it not only denies the spirit but wishes to force spirit into matter. They see that materialism takes forms that can already be denied. People can say that materialism has disappeared and that we are already speaking about spirit, but these are the people who speak of spirit in a vague way. It is very easy to be a materialist when all of nature has been made into spirit in such a way that psychic phenomena emerge. Most important, one is able to look into the concrete spirit world.

Through those seances, these brotherhoods betray themselves, so to speak. Instead of hiding themselves, they have revealed themselves through seances. This shows that their scheme was not quite successful. Consequently, for awhile during the 1890s, the impulse arose within these brotherhoods to discredit spiritism. In other words, you can see how incisive effects can be accomplished this way, using the methods of the spirit world. What we are dealing with here is an enhancement of power—the exploitation of certain evolutionary conditions that must emerge in the course of human evolution.

This growing materialization of human souls, this imprisonment of souls within the earthly sphere (lodges are also in the earthly sphere) will be counteracted. If souls therefore haunt the lodges and are intended to be effective there, they must be confined to the earthly realm. This effort and impulse to work in the earthly sphere through those souls is counteracted by the important impulse of the Mystery of Golgotha. This impulse is also healing the world against the soul's materialization. The way of Christ himself is completely beyond the will and intentions of human beings. Thus, no person, no matter how knowledgeable—even an initiate—can influence the activity of Christ, which during the course of the twentieth century will lead to the appearance I have spoken of and about which you will find indications in my mystery dramas. This event depends completely on Christ himself. Christ will exist in the earthly sphere as an etheric being. It depends on human beings to establish the right relationship with him. Therefore, no one—not the most powerful initiate—has any influence on the appearance of Christ. It will come. I beg you to hold firmly to this. To make it effective, however, arrangements can be made to receive the Christ event in one way or another.

The brotherhoods I just spoke of—those that wish to confine human souls to the materialistic sphere—work toward making the Christ event pass unnoticed in the twentieth century; they would prefer his appearance as etheric being to be unobserved by human beings. This effort evolves under the influence of a very specific idea and impulse of will. These brotherhoods have an urge to conquer the sphere of influence that will come through Christ in the twentieth century, and furthermore, to win it for another being, about whom we will speak in more detail later on. Certain brotherhoods of the West actively battle the Christ impulse. They want to replace the Christ with a being who has never appeared in the flesh, but only as an etheric being with a strong ahrimanic nature.

Ultimately, activities such as those involving the dead serve only to lead people away from Christ, who went through the Mystery of Golgotha; their goal is to allow the earth to be ruled by another being. It is an actual struggle—not just facts that I learned as abstract concepts or whatever, but a real struggle. It is a struggle that wants to replace the Christ being with another in the course of human evolution, for the duration of the fifth, sixth, and seventh post-Atlantean periods. To annihilate such truly anti-Christian efforts will require healthy, honest spiritual development; and that requires clear insight. The brotherhoods

call this other being, whom they wish to substitute as ruler, the
"Christ." They will actually call him Christ, and it will be
important be to distinguish between the true Christ—who will
not be incarnated in the flesh when he appears—and the being
who has never been incarnated on earth. This other being has
never reached beyond etheric embodiment, but the brotherhoods will put him in the place of Christ, whom they hope will
pass by unobserved.

This is the portion of the battle concerned with counterfeit-
ing the appearance of Christ in the twentieth century. Those
who observe life only superficially—especially when discussing
Christ and questions of Jesus and the like—do not see very
deeply. This is the smoke of deception that diverts people from
deeper matters and essential issues. When theologians argue
about Christ, a spiritual influence from somewhere always
enters their discussions. Such people end up encouraging goals
that are very different from those they advocate consciously.

This is exactly the danger inherent in the concept of the
unconscious; people become confused even about these circumstances. The evil brotherhoods pursue their goals very consciously, but of course what they pursue becomes unconscious
for those who speak and plan superficially. One cannot get to
the heart of the matter, however, by speaking about the unconscious, because the so-called unconscious is really on the other
side of the threshold, beyond everyday awareness. It is in a
sphere where the plans of those with knowledge can unfold.
You can see that this is essentially one side of the situation—
that a number of brotherhoods really do take a position of
opposition and wish to replace the activity of Christ with the
activity of another being. These brotherhoods arrange everything for their own purpose.

Countering this activity are brotherhoods of the East (especially Indian brotherhoods), who wish to interfere just as much in human evolution. These Indian brotherhoods pursue a different goal. They never developed the kind of esotericism that would allow them to ensnare the dead within their realm, the realm of the lodges. That is far from their purposes, and they are not interested in such things. On the other hand, neither do they wish the Mystery of the Golgotha and its impulse to take hold of human evolution. This is not because they do not have the dead are at their disposal, as do the brotherhoods of the West. Their goal is not to substitute another being for the Christ, who will enter human evolution as an etheric being during the twentieth century; for that they would need the dead, which they do not have. Instead they want to steer interest away from this Christ. These brotherhoods of the East hope to keep Christianity from becoming strong, especially the Indian brotherhoods. They do not want interest in the true Christ to flourish—the Christ who had only one incarnation for three years on earth, and who cannot appear physically again on earth. They do not wish to use the dead in their lodges, but something other than those who once lived as human beings. In those Eastern lodges of India, a different kind of being is used in place of the dead.

When people die, they leave behind an ether body; as you know, it separates off soon after death. Under normal conditions, the ether body is assimilated by the cosmos. This process is complicated, and I have described it in numerous ways. Before the Mystery of Golgotha, and even after—especially in Eastern regions—something peculiar was a possibility. After death, when human beings surrender the ether body, certain other beings can inhabit it; with the ether bodies laid aside by human beings, they become etheric beings. In Eastern regions, therefore, it happens that not just dead people but all kinds of demonic spirits are induced to inhabit human ether bodies. The demonic spirits that inhabit those etheric bodies are then received into the Eastern lodges. The Western lodges thus receive the dead who have been confined to the material realm; the Eastern lodges of the left receive demonic spirits that do not belong to earthly evolution but creep into earthly evolution by occupying the ether bodies vacated by human beings.

Exoterically, this phenomenon is transformed through veneration. You know that certain brotherhoods possess the art of invoking illusions. Because people are unaware of how common illusion already is, they can be easily deceived by artificially invoked illusions. This is how it is done: one's goals are clothed in veneration. Imagine a tribe or clan of related people; as an "evil" brother, I have made arrangements ahead of time for the ether body of an ancestor to be occupied by a demonic being. I tell those people that they must venerate this ancestor. The ancestor is merely the one who left an ether body, which was then occupied by demons through contrivances of the lodge. The veneration of ancestors is thereby brought about, but the people are simply worshipping the demonic beings who inhabit the ether body of an ancestor.

The worldview of people in the East can be diverted from the Mystery of Golgotha through such methods of the Eastern lodges. As a result, they achieve their purpose—that the Christ, as he passes over the earth, remains unnoticed by people of the East, and perhaps by people everywhere. Thus, they do not wish to substitute a false Christ; they simply want the appearance of Jesus Christ to go unnoticed.

Thus, to a certain extent, a twofold struggle is waged today against the Christ appearing in the etheric during the twentieth century. Humanity is placed into this evolution. Essentially, what we see occurring in individual cases is simply a result of processes and events in the great impulses of human evolution. For that reason, it is sad that people are deceived whenever the so-called unconscious is working within them—owing perhaps to a fading love affair or the like—when, in fact, impulses of extremely conscious spirituality are passing on all sides through humanity. But they remain relatively unconscious if one does not deal with them in one's consciousness. And you must add much more to this. Those who have been honestly concerned with human evolution have always taken these things into consideration, and they have done what was right from their point of view. People really cannot do more than this.

Ireland, during the first Christian centuries, was an excellent shelter for spiritual life—an exceptionally good one, protected against all possible illusions. More than any other region on earth, it was real protection from any possible illusion. This is why so many of those who wished to spread Christianity during its early centuries originated in Ireland. They had to work with a naïve population, however, because the Europeans among whom they worked in those days were somewhat primitive. Whereas they had to consider the naïveté of the people, they themselves had to know and understand the great impulses of humanity.

During the fourth and fifth centuries in particular, Irish initiates were active in Central Europe. They began there while preparing for what would take place in the future. To a certain extent, they were influenced by the initiate knowledge that the fifth post-Atlantean era would begin in the fifteenth century

(in 1413, as you know). They also knew that they had to prepare for a completely new age, that naïve humankind must be
protected for this new period. What could they do at that time
to keep harmful influences from entering this unsophisticated
population, surrounding it with a fence, so to speak? What did
they do?

Evolution was guided by well-informed and honest groups,
so that gradually all oceanic travel was eliminated—the kind of
journeys that had been made previously from the northern
lands to America. Whereas in the past boats had crossed from
Norway to America for certain purposes (I shall say more about
this another time), it was arranged that knowledge of America
would be completely forgotten by the Europeans. Thus the
connection with America was gradually obliterated. By the fifteenth century, Europeans knew nothing of America. This
development was directed in particular by Rome, so that the
connection with America would be gradually lost, and Europeans would be sheltered from American influences. The initiate
monks from Ireland, who had spread Christianity throughout
Europe, were especially involved in this process of protecting
European humanity from American influences.

In ancient times, certain influences were brought from
America; during the beginning of the fifth post-Atlantean
epoch, however, matters were arranged so that Europeans
would remain uninfluenced by America; they knew absolutely
nothing about America and believed that it did not exist. As we
know from history, America was not rediscovered until after
the fifth post-Atlantean period had begun. One fact you probably know is that the history one learns in schools is largely
made up of convenient fables. The story that America was discovered for the first time in 1492 is one such fable. It was

merely rediscovered, and the connections were cleverly concealed for awhile, as they had to be. Again, it is important to know what the situation was and understand the real history. True history states that Europe was "fenced in" for awhile, carefully protected from certain influences that were supposed to be kept out of Europe.

Such facts demonstrate the importance of rejecting "the unconscious" as unconscious; it is, in fact, extremely conscious beyond the threshold of normal human awareness. It is very important for the majority of humankind to learn of certain mysteries. Thus I have done as much as I can do now in public lectures in Zurich.[3] There, as you may know, I have sometimes explained the extent to which history is not comprehended by people through ordinary consciousness—that the substance of history is in fact merely a dream of humanity. Until people become aware of this fact, their views will remain unsound.

People will gradually awaken consciousness through these things. The phenomena that actually take place will demonstrate the truth of the matter, but people must make certain they do not overlook them. People are asleep and move blindly through the facts; they also go blindly and sleeping through tragic catastrophes such as the present one. These are matters that I would like to impress upon your hearts—more from the perspective of history today, and tomorrow I will speak of these issues more explicitly.

I would like to add one more image. First, from our discussion you have seen the tremendous difference that exists between East and West in human evolution. Second, I ask you

---

3. These lectures were given November 6 & 13, 1917; "Behind the Scenes of External Events," in *Individuell Geistwesen und ihr Wirken in der Seele des Menschen* (GA 178, from which lectures 10–12 of this volume were taken).

to consider this: psychoanalysts speak of the subconscious life of the soul, and so on. We do not need to discuss such a vague concept, but it is necessary to comprehend what lies beyond the threshold of consciousness. What is there? It is certain that much can be found beneath the threshold of consciousness. What lies in the subconscious, however, is itself extremely conscious. You must understand the kind of conscious spirituality that exists beyond the threshold of consciousness. You must speak of conscious spirituality beyond the threshold of consciousness, not the "unconscious."

You must begin to understand that there is much about human beings that people know nothing about in their ordinary consciousness. People would be in a terrible situation if, in ordinary consciousness, they had to be aware of all that goes on within them. Just consider how difficult eating and drinking would be if people were to become aware of all the physiological and biological processes that take place after the moment of ingestion. All of this takes place outside of ordinary consciousness. Spirit forces are active everywhere, even in the purely physical. Human beings must eat and drink, however, without waiting to learn what really occurs within them. So much goes on within us, but by far the largest portion of our being remains unconscious—or, rather, subconscious.

The odd thing is that, in every case, the human subconscious is taken possession of by another being. We are not simply a fusion of body, soul, and spirit, carrying within us a soul that is independent of our body. Shortly before birth, another being takes possession of the subconscious portions of a human being. That subconscious being accompanies a person throughout life, from birth to death. Just before birth, it enters and accompanies the human being. One can also describe this being as one that permeates a person in the parts that do not come to ordinary consciousness. This is a very intelligent being who possessed a will akin to the forces of nature; its will is much more closely related to the forces of nature than is human volition. I must emphasize the peculiarity, however: this being would suffer tremendously if, under present conditions, it were to experience death along with the human being. Under present conditions, this being cannot experience death with the human being. Thus it disappears just before death; it must always save itself; it always has the urge to arrange the human life so that it will overcome death. It would be disastrous for human evolution, however, if this being were also able to conquer death—that is, if it were able die with the human being and, in this way, enter the spirit worlds occupied by humankind after death. It must always leave before a human being enters the spirit world after death. Sometimes this is very difficult, and all sorts of complications arise.

Here is the situation: this being, which rules completely in the subconscious, is extremely dependent on the earth as a whole organism. The earth described by geologists, mineralogists, and paleontologists is really not the being of earth at all; it is fully alive. Human beings see only its skeleton, because geologists, mineralogists, and paleontologists describe only its mineral nature, which is the earth's skeleton. If you know no more than this, you know about as much as you would if you were to enter this room and, because of some special capacities for sight, were able to see nothing of this honored company but bones. Imagine entering through that door, and here on these chairs sat nothing but skeletons. Not that you have only bones; I don't expect that of you, but imagine a person fitted with some sort of x-ray device. This is exactly the way geologists see the earth; they see only its skeleton. This earth, however, is not just a skeleton but a living organism, and it sends special forces from its center to every point on the surface, to every territory. Imagine the surface of the earth:

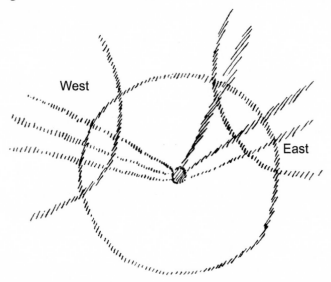

Looking at it on a large scale, you have an Eastern region and a Western region. The forces transmitted from the earth belong to the life organism of the earth itself. Depending on whether people live on one or another place on earth, their immortal souls do not contact these forces directly but only indirectly— the immortal human soul is relatively independent of earthly conditions. The soul depends on earthly conditions only in an artificial way, as was shown today. These various forces work with particular strength, however, along a circuitous path through this other being that takes possession of human beings before birth and must leave before death. These forces affect racial types and geographic differentiations in humankind.

Thus it is this double that human beings carry within them and upon which these geographic locations and other differentiations exert particular influences.[4] This is extremely important, and we will see tomorrow how this double is influenced from various points of the earth, as well as the consequences. I already mentioned that you must consider what I said today along with what will come tomorrow, because they must be understood together.

We must now try to absorb concepts that become even more serious when related to the total reality in which the human soul lives with its entire being. This reality transforms itself in various ways, but the means of this metamorphosis depends greatly upon human beings. Two significant, possible transformations become clear when we understand how human souls imprison themselves on earth or enter the proper spheres, depending on whether they absorb materialistic or spiritual concepts between birth and death. We must become increasingly clear in our concepts about these matters; then we will grow into the correct relationship to the whole world. This will not occur in an abstract spiritual movement; rather, it must happen within us through a spiritual movement of concrete understanding that deals with the spiritual life of a number of beings.

It is truly satisfying for me that such discussions are nurtured here. They are especially important for those among us who are no longer part of the physical plane—those who have passed through the portal of death and remain our faithful members. Such discussions draw us closer to our departed friends.

---

4. See also Rudolf Steiner, *Geographic Medicine* (Mercury Press, 1979), 2 lectures in St. Gallen, Nov. 15–16, 1917 (GA 178).

11 · Spirit Beings and the Ground of the World – 2

Dornach, November 19, 1917

We are currently developing studies related to our efforts toward knowledge that flows in, although, as yet, there are no adequate methods for attaining such knowledge. This has led us to distant historical perspectives, in relation to which I ask you to consider this: we are dealing with reports of real events, not with a theory or system of ideas, but with reports of facts. (This was also true of what was said when I visited last time, with the same intention and impulse.) This is exactly the point we must keep in mind, otherwise it will be difficult to understand these matters.

It is not a matter of developing historical principles or ideas for you, but one of presenting facts that relate to the intentions and purposes of certain individuals who are allied in brotherhoods. They are also allied with beings who influence those brotherhoods—beings whose influence they seek. Such beings are not human or incarnated in the flesh; they are beings that incarnate in the spirit world. You must keep this in mind, especially in regard to what I said yesterday, because in the case of these brotherhoods we are dealing to a certain extent with various factions. You could recognize this in last year's discussion, when I pointed out that, within such brotherhoods, we are dealing with a faction that insists on absolute secrecy regarding certain higher truths.[1] Opposed to them, with various shadings in between, are members of other brotherhoods who contend that, particularly since the middle of the nineteenth century, certain truths must be revealed carefully and appropriately to humanity, even if at first only those truths whose revelation is most necessary. In addition to these main factions, there are other groups with various nuances. From this you can see that what is intended and planted by such brotherhoods as an impulse in human evolution is often subject to compromise.

These brotherhoods were familiar with the spiritual impulses that affect human evolution, and they saw the approach of a significant event at the beginning of the 1840s. That event involved a struggle between certain spirits and higher spirits, which culminated in 1879, when certain angelic spirits of darkness fell prey to an event that is represented symbolically by Michael conquering the dragon. When the brotherhoods sensed this event approaching, they had to take a stand; they had to ask themselves what could be done. The members of brotherhoods that wanted to accommodate the demands of the time were, to some degree, filled with the best intentions. They took up the mistaken impulse that involved the materialism of the time. They considered it preferable to bring something of the spirit world to those who desired only knowledge of the physical path; this was to be communicated directly, using the materialistic way of the physical path. Thus the intentions were good when they thrust spiritism into the world in the 1840s.

---

1. See Rudolf Steiner, *The Karma of Untruthfulness,* especially volume 2 (Rudolf Steiner Press, 1988), 12 lectures in Dornach, Jan. 1–30, 1917 (GA 174).

At the time of this struggle—when the spirit of criticism was to reign on earth, as I have indicated, and the intellect was directed purely to the outer world—it was necessary to give human beings the feeling, at least, that a spirit world surrounds humanity. But compromises arise, and one arose in this case. Members of the brotherhoods who objected completely to revealing certain spiritual truths to humanity felt that they were being beaten by the majority, so to speak, and they had to consent to it. Whenever one deals with a group, and its will prevails, one has to compromise. Naturally, however, whenever something is decided in a group, something is expected to come of that decision—not only by those who instigated it for their own purposes, but also by those who originally opposed the decision.

Well-meaning members of the spiritual brotherhood thus thought incorrectly that, through mediums, people could be convinced of a spirit world surrounding them. They believed that, based on such conviction, it would then be possible to share higher truths with them. This might have worked if the intentions of those well-meaning members had actually taken place—if the revelations of those mediums had been presented as though they were in fact dealing with the surrounding spirit world. However, something completely different took place, as I pointed out yesterday. Those who took part in seances believed that what came to light through the mediums was coming from the dead. Essentially, the revelations of spiritism therefore disappointed everyone. Of course, those who allowed themselves to compromise were most distressed that, during the seances, there was talk about manifestations of departed spirits—at times rightfully. The well-meaning, progressive initiates never expected talk of the dead; they expected to hear mention of the universal elemental world. Thus they were also disappointed.

Such events are followed carefully by those who are initiated in a certain way. In addition to those we mentioned, we have other brotherhoods, or perhaps portions of the same brotherhood, in which minorities (even majorities) could form. We must be aware of other initiates who are called within the brotherhoods "brothers of the left"—in other words, those who exploit for power everything embodied as an impulse in human evolution. It is obvious that the brothers of the left also expected various revelations through spiritism. As I explained yesterday, it was mostly the brothers of the left who arranged to use the souls of people who had died. For them, everything that came out of those seances was of compelling interest. They gradually took over the whole field. The well-meaning initiates gradually lost interest in spiritism; they felt ashamed in a certain sense, because those who were against spiritism from the beginning told them that they should have known right away that nothing could come of spiritism now.

As a result, spiritism entered, as it were, the sphere of power of the brothers of the left. I spoke yesterday about brothers of the left who were disappointed because they saw that spiritism, which had set in motion themselves, revealed the very things they wanted most to keep hidden. Because participants in seances believed they were influenced by the dead, it was possible for messages from the dead to reveal the activities of certain brothers of the left that involved souls of the departed. In those seances, manifestation was possible for souls who had been misused by the brothers of the left.

Keep in mind that, when speaking about these messages, we are not dealing with theories, but facts that can be traced to individuals. When united in brotherhoods, one individual may have an expectation that differs from what another expects from a given situation. It is impossible to speak of realities in the spiritual world; it is impossible to look for anything there but a resolution of the impulses of the individuals. What one does and what another does may come into conflict there, just as it happens life. When theories are discussed, the ground for contradiction may not be broken. But when facts are discussed, it can be shown frequently that those facts agree no more in the spirit world than do the actions of human beings on the physical plane. I therefore ask you always to consider that, when speaking of these things, it is impossible to speak of realities without discussing individual facts. It is these that concern us. Thus it is necessary to keep the individual streams apart—to peel them apart.

This is related with another significant matter, one that, above all, we must become aware of if we wish to gain a satisfying worldview. What I am saying is very important and, although abstract, must be brought before our souls. If we wish to attain such a worldview, we must work toward harmonizing individual aspects of the world. People do this out of habit, which is appropriate since it relates to monotheism, the dearest treasure of human soul and spirit through many centuries. People desire to lead their earthly experiences back to the undivided ground of the world. This is well justified, though not in the way that we usually believe it to be. It is justified in a completely different way, and we will say more about this next time. Today I would like to bring before your souls only what is most important.

Those who approach the world and expect everything to explain itself without contradiction—as though it arose from an undivided ground of the world—will experience many disappointments when facing the world and its experiences without preconceptions. It is traditional for human beings to treat all that they perceive in the world according to a pastoral world-view—one in which everything goes back to the undivided, divine, primordial ground; everything stems from God, so we should be able to understand it as a unity. But this is not true today. The world that surrounds us as experience does not arise from the undivided primordial ground; rather, it stems from a myriad of different spirit beings.

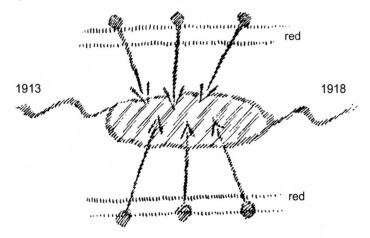

Various beings work together in all that surrounds us in the world as experience. This is mostly the way it is. We will speak next time about other ways of justifying monotheism, but above all, this is the situation. As soon as we cross the threshold of the spirit world, we must think of individual beings to a certain degree—indeed, very much so—as independent of one another. We cannot expect what appears there be subject to an undivided principle. Imagine that this schematic representation is an experience (see drawing); as far as I am concerned, it encompasses experiences between 1913 and 1918.

Of course, the experiences of humankind continue in both directions. Historians are always tempted to assume a unified principle in this whole process, but this is not the case. As soon as we cross into the spirit world—it makes no difference whether one crosses from above or below (red)—various beings work together to influence events that are otherwise relatively independent of one another (arrows). Unless you take this into consideration, you will expect an undivided ground of the world everywhere, and you will never understand those events. Unless you consider a certain ebb and flow in events—variations in the beings who work with or against one another—you will not understand these things correctly.

This is, in fact, related to the deepest mysteries of human evolution. A monotheistic feeling, however, has veiled this fact for centuries or millennia, but it must be considered. Thus, if you wish to progress today in questions of a worldview, above all you must not confuse logic with an abstract absence of contradiction. An abstract lack of contradiction cannot exist in a world where beings work together as well as independently. Thus efforts toward conformity will always lead to impoverished concepts; such concepts cannot encompass full reality. Unless concepts can take hold of a world full of contradictions, which is reality, they be unable to encompass reality as a whole.

The realm of nature that confronts us materializes in a remarkable way. Various beings also work together in all that we call nature, including natural science, nature worship, esthetics of nature, and so on. In the present evolutionary cycle of humanity, however, a fortunate arrangement has been found for humankind through the wise guidance of the world; human beings can comprehend nature through concepts that connect them to undivided guidance. This is because, unless something depends on undivided guidance, it cannot approach human beings as an experience of nature through sensory perception.

Something very different lies beyond the tapestry of nature whose influences are completely different; but it is blocked out in a person's perception of nature. Consequently, what people call nature appears to be a unified system, but only because it has been filtered. When we perceive through the senses, nature is filtered for us, so to speak. Everything contradictory in nature is filtered out, and nature is transmitted to us as an undivided system. Crossing the threshold, however, one perceives reality and becomes clear about nature—the elemental spirits or the influences on human souls that could also be regulated by nature—and one can no longer describe nature as an undivided system. Instead, one becomes clear that we are dealing with the influences of beings that are either struggling with one another or supporting and strengthening one another.

In the elemental world, we find gnome-like spirits of earth, undine-like spirits of water, sylph-like spirits of air; and salamander-like spirits of fire. They are all there. Their task, however, is not to form a working unit; it doesn't work like that. These various realms—those of gnomes, undines, sylphs, and salamanders—are independent in a sense.

These beings, however, do not simply work as cogs in a single system, but struggle with one another. Initially, their intentions have nothing to do with one another, but the effect that arises comes through the way their diverse intentions interact and work together. If one becomes familiar with those intentions, it may be possible to see through the appearances to the interactions of fire spirits and undines. One must never believe, however, that there is some being behind these spirits giving them various commands. This is not the case. This is a common notion today, promoted by philosophers such as Wilhelm Wundt, whom Fritz Mauthner unjustly called an "authority by the grace of his publisher," though he was the authority for almost the whole world before the war.[2] The aim is to unify all that lives in the human soul as cognition, feelings, and volition. They say that the soul is a unity, and therefore everything about the soul must be a unified, common system. This is not so, however, and those significant and powerful contradictions that analytical psychology has discovered could not emerge if our life of thinking beyond the threshold did not lead us back into very different regions where other beings influence our thinking, feeling, and willing.

It is all so strange. You see, here is a human being (see drawing) with a life of thinking, life of feeling, and life of willing (*t, f, w*). A systematizer like Wundt could not imagine anything except that it is a system. The life of thinking leads to one world (*w1*), the life of feeling into another world (*w2*), and the life of willing to yet another world (*w3*), all at the same time.

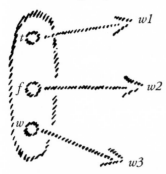

The whole purpose of the human soul is to form a unity of what was, in a momentarily pre-human world, a threefoldness. All these things must be considered whenever we are concerned with the historic impulses of human evolution—impulses that will become part of historic evolution.

I have mentioned in these studies that every era of the post-Atlantean age has a certain purpose. I have characterized, in a general way, the purpose of the fifth post-Atlantean era, saying

2. Wilhelm (Max) Wundt (1832–1920), a German physiologist and psychologist who wrote on the nerves and senses and on the relationships between physiology and psychology.

that it is humanity's task during this period to come to grips with evil as an impulse in world evolution. We have frequently discussed what this implies. The only possibility is that the forces that appear at the wrong place manifest as evil. They can be conquered for humanity, however, through the exertions of human beings in the fifth post-Atlantean period. With these forces of evil, therefore, something good for the future evolution of the whole world is in place to unfold. Consequently, the purpose of the fifth post-Atlantean period is especially difficult. You can see that a great many temptations face humanity. As evil powers gradually appear, it is natural that human beings are more likely, under the circumstances, to surrender to that evil in every realm, while avoiding the struggle to allow the appearance of evil to be given a beneficial role in world evolution. Yet this must happen: evil must be placed, to a degree, at the service of goodness in world evolution. Without this, it would be impossible to enter the sixth post-Atlantean period, which will have a completely different purpose. Its task will be to allow humanity to live, above all, in a constant contemplation of the spirit world, despite the fact that it is still connected with earth. It is exactly this task in the fifth post-Atlantean period—that of opposing evil—that is connected with a certain new possibility of personal darkening for humankind.

We know that since 1879 the spirits of darkness who are closest to human beings—those of the angelic realm—wander the human world, because they were cast out of the spiritual world into the human world and now work through human impulses. Because of this very situation, beings close to humankind work invisibly among human beings who, because of active evil forces, are prevented from recognizing spirit through the intellect. Again, this is connected with the purpose of the fifth post-Atlantean period, and because of this, numerous opportunities occur for the fifth post-Atlantean period to give itself over to dark illusions and such. During this time, people must get used to comprehending spirit through the intellect. Spirit will have been revealed, and because the spirits of darkness were overthrown in 1879, spiritual wisdom can flow increasingly from spirit worlds. If the spirits of darkness had remained above in the spiritual kingdom, they would have hindered that flow, but they can no longer block the flow of spiritual wisdom. They can, however, cause confusion and darken souls, and we have often described the means of exploiting such opportunities. And we have mentioned the methods used to prevent human beings from attaining a spiritual life.

Naturally, none of this should lead to lamenting the facts, but should strengthen the force and energy of human souls to approach the spirit. If in this fifth post-Atlantean period, people can achieve whatever is possible by embodying the forces of evil in a good way; at the same time, something tremendous will be achieved. Thus the fifth post-Atlantean period will understand something for human evolution—ideas greater than those of any other period in earthly evolution. Through the Mystery of Golgotha, for example, Christ appeared during the fourth post-Atlantean period. Only the fifth period, however, can claim this mystery for its own through the human intellect. During the fourth post-Atlantean period, people could understand that they possessed something through the Christ impulse that would lead their souls beyond death; it became clear enough through Pauline Christianity.

This must be kept firmly in mind by those who speak of the spirit world during this fifth post-Atlantean period. Consequently, there are certain matters in this period that can only be spoken of, but speaking is just as important as something else was in another era. In our time, for example, communicating truths (or more trivially, lecturing about truths) is most important. After this, people must find their direction in freedom. People should not go beyond speaking truths; the rest should follow through free resolve, just as events follow resolutions made from impulses of the phenomenal world. This is also related to matters that, to a certain extent, can be directed only from the spirit world. We can understand this better if we go into individual examples.

During the fourth post-Atlantean period, it was still possible to consider matters other than through mere communication. What was considered? A specific example involved Ireland, as we call it today. It had particular characteristics and is distinct from the rest of earth in certain ways. Each part of the earth differs from the others in certain ways. This is not special, therefore I will emphasize only the island's more prominent characteristics, which contrast with other areas of the earth. In earthly evolution (as we have seen in my *Outline of Esoteric Science*), one can look back in time, and various influences and events confirm facts gathered from the spirit world. From that book, you know what existed during the so-called time of Lemuria, as well as various developments since that time. I pointed out yesterday that the whole earth must be considered essentially an organism, from which various forces flow out to the inhabitants of this or that region. This flow has a particular effect on the double, which I spoke of yesterday.

In the past, some of those who were familiar with Ireland expressed its particular characteristics in fairy tales and legends. I would like to point to an esoteric legend that expresses the essence of Ireland in relation to the earthly organism. It was said that humankind was cast from paradise because Lucifer had misled humanity there, and people were thus scattered across the rest of the world. The rest of the world, however, was already there when humanity was forced to leave paradise. Thus, one can distinguish (according to this fairy tale) between the paradise of Lucifer and the rest of earth, into which humanity was expelled. In this sense, Ireland is not part of earth; before Lucifer entered paradise, its likeness had formed on the earth and became Ireland. But something even more meaningful will enter evolution during the fifth post-Atlantean period; human souls will recognize that Christ is their helper in transforming evil forces into benevolent forces.

Something related to this characteristic of the fifth post-Atlantean period should be inscribed each day in our souls. Although people tend to forget this, it should always be remembered that we must become fighters for the spirit during this post-Atlantean period. People must realize that their forces will become weak unless they continually hold them for the conquest of the spirit world. People are given the greatest freedom in the fifth post-Atlantean period, and they must accept this. To a certain degree, the idea of human freedom must become the testing ground for all that humanity encounters during the fifth post-Atlantean period. If human forces weaken, everything could take a turn for the worse. During this period, people are not to be led like children. There are certain brotherhoods, however, whose ideal is to lead people like children, just as they were during the third and fourth post-Atlantean periods. Those brotherhoods are not doing what needs to be done for human evolution: directing humankind toward spirit in such a way that acceptance or rejection of the spirit world is a free choice of each individual.

You should fully understand that Ireland is the area of earth that had nothing to do with Lucifer. It would have prevented Lucifer from entering paradise, therfore Ireland had to be separate so that an earthly likeness of paradise would arise. According to legend, Ireland was a separate area that would have hindered Lucifer from entering paradise. Lucifer could not enter paradise until Ireland had been separated from it.

This very beautiful esoteric legend (related here in a very incomplete way) explained for many people the unique purpose of Ireland over the centuries. In the first mystery drama I wrote ("The Portal of Initiation") you find the familiar story of how Europe was originally Christianized by Irish monks. When St. Patrick introduced Christianity to Ireland, conditions were such that Christianity led to great devotion. This legend is given new meaning by the fact that, in those times, Ireland (called *Ierne* by the Greeks, and *Ivernia* by the Romans) was called the Isle of the Saints. The best impulses of European Christianity originated directly from Ireland—from Irish people, lovingly initiated into Christianity. It was called this because of the great devotion that prevailed in their Christian cloisters. This is related to the fact that the territorial forces I mentioned rose from earth and took hold of the human double. Such forces are at their very best in Ireland.

You might say, therefore, that Ireland must be home to the best people. This is true, but not the best in the world. Into every region Other people wander into every region and leave descendants and so on. Human beings, therefore, are not merely the product of the piece of earth on which they stand. The forces ascending from earth may also oppose the character of those who live there. Do not confuse the way people actually develop with the characteristics of the earthly organism in a given region. This would only open you once more to the world of illusion.

We can say today, however, that Ireland is a special land. Out of this, one fact among many should emerge and lead us to fruitful social and political ideas; we must consider these facts. What I said about Ireland is a fact, and we must deal with such facts. We must bring everything together and create a science that deals with the way human conditions form on earth. Until this happens, no real healing can come into the structure of public affairs. Communications from the spirit world must flow into the legislation we encounter. Consequently, I have said in public lectures that it is important for everyone involved in public affairs (government officials and so on) to become familiar with such matters. This is the only way that public servants can get a hold on reality. They will not do this (at least not yet), but it is needed, nevertheless.

In keeping with the purpose of the fifth post-Atlantean period, we must emphasize communication, because judgment is needed before such matters can become action, and actions are determined by impulses in the physical world. The situation was different in the past, when people were able to act through different means. At a definite moment during the third post-Atlantean era, one brotherhood arranged to send a large number of colonists from Asia Minor to the Irish island. At the time, colonists were settled in the Asian region that would later give birth to the philosopher Thales, about whom you may read in my *Riddles of Philosophy*.[3] Thales came from

3. Thales of Miletus (c.625–547 B.C.), the Greek philosopher who gained fame in his day by predicting solar eclipses. Aristotle considered him the father of Greek philosophy. See *The Riddles of Philosophy* (Anthroposophic Press, 1973; GA 18), pp. 24ff.

that region later on; he was not born, of course, until the fourth post-Atlantean period. Earlier, initiates sent colonists to Ireland—out of the spiritual substance from which Thales arose. Why? Because they were familiar with the characteristics of an earthly region such as Ireland; they knew what that eso-teric legend indicated. They knew that the forces ascending from the earth through the soil of Ireland affected people in such a way that they were not influenced much in the direction of intellectuality, egoism, and analysis. The initiates who sent colonists there were fully aware of this, and they selected those who, because of their particular karmic predisposition, seemed well-suited to the influences of Ireland. Descendants of that old population from Asia Minor still live in Ireland today—people who were intended to develop special qualities of the feeling soul rather than intellectuality and judgment.

Through these events, Christianity evolved gloriously in Ire-land and spread peacefully, leading to the Christianization of Europe. This was prepared far in advance. The compatriots of Thales later sent people to Ireland, and they proved capable of becoming monks and working there as I described. Such things were often done in ancient times, and when such colonies are described by today's ignorant historians (who are very intelli-gent in the common sense), you must understand that within such colonizations there is deep wisdom, directed and guided by knowledge of what would occur in the future through earthly evolution. This was another way of bringing spiritual wisdom into the world. Those who are on the proper path, however, should not do this today. It would be wrong to parti-tion the earth by requiring people to do something that is against their will; rather one should simply tell the truth so that people can guide themselves accordingly.

You can see that this was an essential progression from the third to the fifth post-Atlantean periods. Keep this clearly in view and see how this impulse toward freedom must work its way through everything that prevails during the fifth post-Atlantean period. The "antagonist" conspires exactly against any feeling of human freedom. That antagonist is the double that accompanies individuals from the time just before birth until just before death, when it must abandon them. If a person is influenced directly by the double, all sorts of things might emerge even during the fifth post-Atlantean period. It is inappropriate during this period, however, for people to be given the full possibility of achieving their purpose, which is the struggle to transform evil into goodness.

Just consider what lies behind the human situation in the fifth post-Atlantean period. Individual facts must be illuminated in the right way and understood, for wherever the double focuses its work, it goes against the essential orientation of the fifth post-Atlantean period. In this period, humanity has not progressed far enough to evaluate the facts correctly. Especially during these recent sad three years [of World War], humankind has not been at all ready to assess the facts in the right way.

Let us take a fact, however, that seems quite unrelated to what I have discussed today. There is a large iron factory, and ten thousand tons of molten iron had to be loaded onto trains. Of course, a certain number of workers must be engaged for such a job—at least seventy-five, it turned out, since each could load twelve and a half tons per day. There was one man, Taylor, who put more emphasis on the double than on what must be gained for humanity in the sense of progress and for the human spirit during the fifth post-Atlantean period. He began by asking the factory owners if they doubted that one man could load much more than twelve and a half tons per day. The factory owners thought that a worker could load at most eighteen tons. Then Taylor said, "Let's experiment."

He began to experiment with the workers. A machine standard was applied to human society, since these experiments involved human beings. He tested to see if what the practical factory owners had said was true—that a man could load no more than eighteen tons a day. He arranged for rest periods, which he calculated physiologically; during these intervals, the workers would recoup all the forces they had exerted. Naturally, it turned out that under these conditions the results differed from one worker to another. Then he worked it out mathematically. You know that it makes no difference if we use mathematical methods in mechanics, but with human beings we cannot use such means, because each person has a unique purpose in life. Taylor employed mathematical means, however: he selected those who recovered completely during the rational pauses, and he granted them those pauses. The others were unable to regain their forces during these rest periods, so they were simply eliminated. By experimenting with people in this way, it was discovered that the selected workers who recovered completely during the breaks could each load forty-seven and a half tons.

He applied the mechanics of Darwin's theory to the life of workers: out with the unfit, while the fit are selected. The fit are those who, fully utilizing their breaks, could load not a maximum of eighteen tons, as had been assumed earlier, but forty-seven and a half tons. In this way, the workers were also satisfied, because immense savings allowed the wages for each remaining worker to be increased sixty per cent. The chosen ones are thus those best adapted to the struggle for existence;

they were chosen through natural selection, and very satisfied besides—although, the unfit may starve to death.

This is the beginning of a principle. Such matters are not easily recognized, because they are not illuminated by larger perspectives; we must elucidate these ideas with a broader view. Today, it is wrong to apply the ideas of natural science to human life. But this impulse continues and will be applied to esoteric truths in the fifth post-Atlantean period. Darwinism is without esoteric truths and will lead to great monstrosities if its views are used to experiment with human beings. Esoteric truths must be revealed during the fifth post-Atlantean era, and if they are added to Darwinian views, an incredible power will be gained over human beings through selection of the fittest. In addition to selecting the fit, there will be efforts toward an eso-teric invention to adapt the fit to be even more fit, which will lead to a tremendous exploitation of power that will oppose the good tendencies of the fifth post-Atlantean period.

I spoke of these relationships to show you the intentions for the future that are just beginning, and to demonstrate the need to illuminate these matters from a higher view. Next time we will point out three or four great truths that must be com-prehended during the fifth post-Atlantean period. It will be shown how these truths can be misused if not applied in a good way today, but are used instead to meet the demands of the double, which are supported by the brotherhoods wishing to replace the Christ with another being.

12 · Spirit Beings and the Ground of the World – 3

Dornach, November 25, 1917

Today I would like to connect and amplify certain observations in our studies with various details. If you attentively follow the times, you may have noticed here and there that people can no longer find help for the future in the thoughts, experiences, and impulses that seem to have brought humankind so much wonderful progress. Yesterday, one of our members gave me last week's *Frankfurter Zeitung*, dated November 21, 1917. In that issue is an article by a very learned gentleman—he has been very well educated, because next to his name was not only the title Doctor of Philosophy but also Doctor of Theology and Professor. As professor, doctor of theology, and doctor of philosophy, he is of course very smart. His article deals with all sorts of contemporary spiritual needs. In this article there is a section that expresses the following:

> The experience of being that lies behind phenomena has no need of pious ceremony or religious judgment, because it is religion itself. Here it is not a matter of the feeling and comprehension of one's own values, but of that great Irrational hidden behind all existence. One who touches it so that the divine spark leaps across, has an experience that is

the primary, "primeval" experience. To experience this, along with all that is moved by the same stream of life, endows one with (to use a word beloved today) a cosmic feeling for life.

Forgive me, dear friends. I am not reading this to arouse lofty images within you in response to such clichés; I wish only to present a sign of our time. "A cosmic religiousness is now growing among us, and the extent that people long for it is demonstrated by the visible growth of the theosophical movement, which attempts to discover and reveal the movement of life beyond the senses." It is indeed difficult to get through all these clichés, but isn't it true that, as a sign of the time, this is peculiar? Further on he says, "In this cosmic piety, it is not a matter of mysticism that first rejects the world..." and so on.

It is difficult to find anything intelligent in these sentences. Since the professor, doctor of theology, and doctor of philosophy states it, however, one must naturally assume it is intelligent. Otherwise, one would have to see it as a clumsily expressed and vague tirade—something that reminds us of an ignorant gentleman who cannot continue traveling along a path and feels the need to point to something, so that matters do not seem completely hopeless. One should not find delight in such statements, and they must not lull us to sleep merely because we notice that somewhere, someone has once again noticed that something lies behind the movement of spiritual science. This would be very detrimental, because those who say such things are often the very ones who are satisfied by the words and go no further. Such people even use these clichés to indicate an event that will come into the world. These are exactly the ideas of those who are too comfortable to become involved in anything that requires a serious study of spiritual science.

This event must truly break in and take hold of human feeling, so that everything related to this reality can flow into evolution and bring healing forces. Of course, it is easier to talk about "surging waves" and "cosmic feelings" than it is to seriously go into all that is required by the signs of our time, which must be made known to humankind. Consequently, it seems we must say things here that have been stated before in public lectures; but now we will speak further and emphasize the difference between what is worn out and lifeless and has brought us to these catastrophic times, and what must now take hold of the human soul if any progress is to be made.

With the old wisdom that humanity used to reach the present, thousands of congresses can be held—world congresses, national congresses, whatever—and thousands of societies can be established, but we must be clear that such congresses and societies will have no effect if the spiritual lifeblood of spiritual science does not flow through them. What people lack today is the courage to truly explore the spirit world. It sounds odd, but all it takes to begin, for example, is the publication and broad circulation of a small brochure such as "Human Life in the Light of Spiritual Science."[1] This would accomplish something new by calling forth knowledge of humanity's connection with the cosmic order; this brochure focuses precisely on such knowledge. It concretely points out how the earth alters its conditions of consciousness each year and so on. The lecture in this brochure gives full consideration to the needs of our time in particular. Receiving this would have more meaning than all the vague talk of cosmic feeling

---

1. Rudolf Steiner, "Human Life in the Light of Spiritual Science" (Anthroposophic Press, 1938), a lecture in Liestal, Switzerland, Oct. 16, 1916 (GA 35).

and about entering some sort of surging waves and so on. I had to quote these things to you, because I was unable to paraphrase them; the ideas are just too senseless. One is not hindered, of course, by noticing these things, since they are important and essential. What I want to emphasize is that we must not mystify, but clarify. Complete clarity is needed to work for anthroposophic spiritual science.

As I have pointed out before, during the fifth post-Atlantean period, it is essential for humanity to approach, in a particular way, the great issues of life that have been obscured in a way through past knowledge. One such issue can be described this way: people will have to try to place the spiritual etheric in the service of ordinary practical life. I pointed out that the fifth post-Atlantean period must resolve the problem of how human moods and emotions allow themselves to be translated into technological wave activity—how humankind must become increasingly connected with mechanisms. Thus a week ago I focused a bit on how this mechanization will be found acceptable by those in certain regions of the earth. I gave an example of how American thinking led to an attempt to extend technology over human life itself. I also gave an example of workers' breaks being exploited so that some of the workers increased their output to fifty tons; one only has to apply the Darwinian principle of natural selection to human life.

In such cases, there is a desire to harness human energy to mechanical energy. This should not be countered by fighting it; that approach would not work at all. These kinds of things will certainly appear. Our concern is whether such innovations are entrusted to those who are familiar with the great goals of earthly evolution in a selfless way and who structure matters for the benefit of human beings, or whether they are accomplished by groups of people who exploit events only in the interest of themselves or a particular group; this is the important issue. It is not a matter of whether this happens; it is sure to come. It is really a question of how one deals with these situations. These events themselves are simply part the purpose of earthly evolution. The unification of human nature and technology will be a significant problem for the rest of earthly evolution.

I have frequently made it a point, even in public lectures, to state that human consciousness is related to that of disintegration. Twice in public lectures in Basel, I said that we are in the process of dying within our nervous system.[2] These forces of dying will become increasingly powerful, and a bond will be established between these forces, which are related to electromagnetism and external mechanistic forces. Human beings will, to a certain extent, "become their intentions," they will be able to direct thoughts into mechanical forces. Previously unknown forces in human nature will be discovered—forces that will be able to affect external electromagnetic forces.

The first challenge related to this will be to unite human beings with technology, which must become an increasingly dominant factor in the future. The second problem involves calling for help from the spiritual situation. But this can be done only when the time is ripe and enough people have been prepared properly. Eventually, however, spiritual forces will be made flexible enough to master sickness and death; medicine will become intensely spiritualized. Caricatures of these facts come from certain sources, but they do show what must in fact happen. Again, there is the possibility that this problem will be

---

2. Steiner may be referring to his lectures of October 18–19, 1917 in Basel; they are not listed in *Gesammelte Aufsätze* (GA).

approached from the same direction I mentioned before: purely out of self-interest or for the benefit of only a particular group. The third matter will be to actually introduce human thinking into human evolution, at birth and through education. I have pointed out that conferences have already taken place to establish a materialistic science that deals with conception and the relationships between men and women.

All these things show us that something significant is developing. It is still easy to say, "Why aren't these things applied by those who understand such matters in the right way?" In the future, it will become clear exactly which forces continue to hinder the foundation of a widespread spiritualized medicine or national economy. For now, we can only talk about these things, until people have enough understanding and are ready to accept the situation selflessly. Today, many people believe that they are able to do this, but many circumstances of life hinder what they are able to do. These circumstances in life cannot be overcome in the right way until a deeper understanding gains ground and there is willingness to renounce, at least temporarily, any immediate, practical application of such things on a large scale.

Matters have developed in such a way that, until the fourteenth and fifteenth centuries, little was retained of what was once hidden behind the ancient, atavistic paths. People talk a lot today about ancient alchemy. Processes such as the procreation of a Homunculus, for example, are also discussed at times, but such talk is mostly groundless. With some understanding of the Homunculus scene in Goethe's *Faust*, one would be better informed about such things; basically, since the sixteenth century, these matters have been shrouded in a kind of fog and have receded from human consciousness.

The principle behind this is the same as the law that regulates the inner human rhythm of waking and sleeping. Human beings cannot rise above sleep, and similarly, in spiritual evolution, we cannot disregard the sleep of spiritual science that has marked the time since the sixteenth century. It has been necessary for humanity to be asleep to the spirit for awhile, so that spiritual knowledge could reappear in a different form. People must comprehend such necessities without becoming discouraged by them. Consequently, we must be very clear that the time has come for awaking and that we must take an active role in this process. Events often hurry ahead of understanding, and you will not comprehend the events around you unless you become familiar with the necessary facts.

As I have repeatedly pointed out, certain egoistic groups are at work esoterically, and their influence is active in the ways that I have often indicated in these studies. First, certain knowledge had to recede within humanity—knowledge called by such misunderstood terms as alchemy and astrology. This knowledge had to fall into a kind of sleep so that human beings could no longer comprehend soul by observing nature, but would have to become more self-reliant. As a result, people can awaken the forces within, because it was necessary for certain things to appear first as abstract concepts and then, later on, assume concrete, spiritual form.

Three ideas have gradually arisen in evolution during recent centuries—ideas that have entered human life as essentially abstract. Kant has named them incorrectly, whereas Goethe gave them the correct names. Kant called these ideas "God," "freedom," and "immortality." Goethe called them "God," "virtue," and "immortality." When we see what is concealed behind these words, it becomes clear that they do not differ from abstract modern ideas that were seen in more concrete ways until the fourteenth and fifteenth centuries. In the ancient atavistic sense, they were also seen in a more material way. They experimented in the ancient way—indeed, using alchemical experiments, they tried to see the activity of God in processes; they tried to produce the "philosopher's stone."

Something real is hidden behind all these things. This philosopher's stone was intended to give people an opportunity to become virtuous, but it was viewed materialistically. It was intended to lead humankind to immortality, to position people in a particular relationship to the cosmos, through which they would have an inner experience of what goes beyond birth and death. All these clichéd ideas that are used today to comprehend ancient things no longer accord with their original meaning. Modern humanity speaks out of ideas that have become abstract. People have wanted to understand God through abstract theology; the idea of virtue has also become purely abstract. The more abstract the idea, the better modern people like to use it when speaking of these things—even immortality. People speculate about what might be immortal in human beings. I spoke about this in my first lecture in Basel, saying that when science concerns itself philosophically with immortality, it is undernourished. It becomes merely another way of expressing abstract thinking about such questions.

Certain brotherhoods in the West, however, have preserved their relationship with the old traditions, and they have tried to apply them in relevant ways by placing them in the service of their common egoism. It is indeed necessary to point this out. Naturally, when people in the West speak publicly about these things in exoteric literature, then "God," "virtue" (or "freedom"), and "immortality" are discussed in the abstract. Only within a circle of initiates is it known that this is all merely speculation and abstractions. Initiates look for something much more concrete than the abstract formulas of God, virtue, and immortality. Consequently, these terms are translated for the initiates in their various schools: God becomes "gold," and one looks behind the question to arrive at the mystery of gold. Gold represents all that is like the sun within the earth's crust; indeed, within gold is imbedded a very meaningful mystery. Gold has the same physical relationship to other substances that "thinking the thought of God" has to other thoughts. It only matters how one understands this mystery.

This is related to the egoistic group exploitation of the mystery of birth. One struggles here with real cosmic understanding. Modern humankind has completely replaced this cosmic understanding with a terrestrial understanding. For example, when people today want to examine how embryos in animals and human beings develop, they look through a microscope at a tiny spot with a microscopic eye; it is thought that this is really the object of examination, but it cannot be limited to this. It will be discovered (and some are getting close to discovering this) that the active forces are not those that meet the microscopic eye; rather, they stream in from cosmic constellations. When an embryo comes into being, it does so because active forces from every direction in the cosmos flow into the living being in which the embryo is forming. When fertilization occurs, embryonic development depends on variations in the activities of cosmic forces.

There is one thing that will come to be understood today that is not yet known. Consider some living being—say, a chicken. When a new embryo arises in this living being, a biologist may examine how an egg grows from the chicken. One

examines the forces that supposedly allow the egg to grow out
of the chicken, but this is nonsense. The egg does not grow
from the hen, which is only a foundation; the forces for that
growth work in from the cosmos and produce the egg on the
foundation prepared within the hen. When modern biologists
work with microscopes, they believe that what they see
includes the forces behind what they are looking at. What they
see, however, is ruled by starry forces that work together in a
constellation. When one discovers the cosmos at work here, the
truth is also discovered; indeed, it is the universe that brings the
egg from the hen. All of this is connected mostly with the mystery of the sun and, from an earthly perspective, with the mystery of gold. Today I am offering only a kind of systematic
indication; with time, it will become clearer.

In the schools we were talking about, virtue is not called "virtue," but simply "health," and they try to become familiar with
the cosmic constellations related to human health and illness.
By acquainting oneself with the cosmic constellations, however, one learns the individual substances on the earth's surface
(liquids and such) that relate to health and illness. Certain
approaches are increasingly developing a more materialistic science of health, but based on a spiritual foundation.

This approach will also lead to the widespread notion that
people become good not by learning ethical principles, but by
ingesting, say, copper under one constellation of stars or arsenic
under another.[3] You can imagine how such things could be
exploited for power by groups of egoists. It is necessary only to
withhold such knowledge from those unable to participate,

3. Here Steiner is referring to homeopathic types of remedies. See, for example,
Rudolf Steiner, *Introducing Anthroposophical Medicine* (Anthroposophic Press,
1999), lecture 7.

which is the best method of ruling great masses of people. One need not speak of these things at all, but only introduce, for example, some new delicacy. People search the markets for this new, appropriately tinged delicacy, and thus accomplish what is necessary from a materialistic perspective. We must be clear that, within all phenomena, there are hidden spiritual activities. Only those who truly know that nothing is material—that all is spirit—will penetrate beyond the mysteries of life.

You can see outer indications of all of this. Perhaps some of you have noticed a book that caused a brief sensation, a book from the West titled *Der Unfug des Sterbens* (*The Nuisance of Dying*).[4] Things all move in this direction, and this is just the beginning. It has gone beyond the way it began, and groups carefully keep it esoteric for their own self-interest. These things become possible when people channel such things materialistically, making abstract ideas of God, virtue, and immortality into concrete ideas of gold, health, and prolonging physical life—by exploiting group egoism with what I presented as the great problems of the fifth post-Atlantean era. What our professor, doctor of theology, doctor of philosophy calls "cosmic feeling" in a clichéd way, is presented as cosmic knowledge by many (often in an egoistic way, unfortunately).

For centuries, science has viewed only those processes occurring on earth, and it has rejected any study of what is approaching as the most important extraterrestrial event. However, it will be precisely during this fifth post-Atlantean time that science will consider exploiting those forces penetrating from the cosmos. Today it is especially important for ordinary

---

4. Prentice Mulford, *Der Unfug des Sterbens. Ausgewählte Essays, bearbeitet und aus dem Englischen übersetzt von Sir Galahad* (München: Langen 1909). His essays are available in English as *The Gift of the Spirit* (Gordon Press, 1981).

professors of biology to begin looking through much-enlarged microscopes, to use more exact laboratory methods. Likewise, in the future, when science becomes spiritualized, it will be important to distinguish between one's activities in the morning, evening, or at noon, or whether to allow one's morning activities to be somehow affected by active influences in the evening, or whether the cosmic influence of morning until evening is to be excluded, or immobilized. In the future such processes will prove necessary, and they will take place. Of course, a lot of water will run over the dam before materialistically minded university chairs, laboratories, and the like are handed over to spiritual science, but this exchange must take place if humanity is avoid complete decadence.

Today's laboratory work will have to be replaced. For example, in the future, when it is a matter of accomplishing something beneficial for the future, certain processes will take place in the morning and be interrupted during the day; in the evening, the cosmic stream passes through them again, and this is preserved rhythmically until it is morning again. These processes will be conducted so that certain cosmic affects are always interrupted during the day, and the cosmic processes of morning and evening are studied. To achieve this, many arrangements will be needed. Likewise, there will be an attempt in this way to channel the question of immortality into materialistic methods. This problem of immortality can be directed in materialistic way by similarly exploiting cosmic constellations. Of course, one does not attain what is often thought of as immortality, but a different immortality. As long as it is impossible to prolong life artificially by influencing the physical body, one will undergo soul experiences that make it possible to remain in the lodge of a brotherhood, even after death, to help them through the forces at one's disposal. In these groups, immortality is simply called "prolonging life."

You can understand from this that, when one is not able to participate publicly in events, one can only talk about them. Those who prefer gold, health, and prolonged life over God, virtue, and immortality do not work with the processes of morning and evening, but with something totally different. As I mentioned last time, there was the intention to eliminate the impetus of the Mystery of Golgotha from the world by introducing another from the West, a kind of antichrist. From the East there are efforts to paralyze the Christ impulse in the twentieth century by directing the attention away from Christ's appearance in the etheric.

Those concerned with introducing this antichrist have tried to exploit something that could work through the most materialistic forces, yet work spiritually with those forces. Most of all, they wish to influence the entire earth by exploiting electricity and the earth's magnetic force. I have shown you how earthly forces arise in the human double; this is a mystery that will be understood. It will be an American mystery that employs the "double" of earth's magnetic force, both north and south, to guide forces that work spiritually around the world. Look at a map of the earth's magnetic force and compare it to what I am saying. Follow a line along which a compass needle swings to an east-west orientation and one where it does not move at all (I can give you only indications for now). Spirit beings are constantly active from a certain celestial direction. One need only put those spirit beings in the service of earthly existence. Because they direct their work in from the cosmos, they are able to communicate the secret of the earth's magnetic force, making it possible to comprehend the mystery of the earth's magnetism. Thus, those groups whose only concern is self-interest can bring about very significant events in relation to gold, health, and prolonged life. It will simply be a matter of mustering the shady boldness. This will be accomplished in certain groups.

In the East, it is a matter of strengthening what I have already described: the influx of active beings from opposing sides of the cosmos are made to serve earthly existence, and in the future a great struggle will arise. Human science will become more oriented toward the cosmos, but in different ways. The benevolent purpose of healing science will be to find cosmic forces that can work on earth through the interactions of two cosmic streams, those of Pisces and Virgo. The most important task will be to penetrate the secret of how forces coming from Pisces (as sun forces) combine with those from Virgo. Good will come from discovering how the morning and evening forces—coming from these two directions of the cos-mos—can serve humanity, on the one hand, from the direction of Pisces, and on the other, from Virgo.

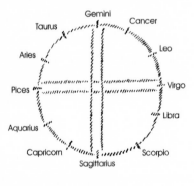

Those who which to work through the polarity of positive and negative forces will not be concerned with these forces. The spiritual mysteries that allow spirit to flow from the cos-mos (through forces of positive and negative magnetism) emerge from Gemini as midday forces. The ancients knew that this is related in some way with the cosmos, and even today it is known to conventional science that positive and negative magnetic forces are somehow hidden behind Gemini in the zodiac. An attempt will be made to paralyze what should be gained through the revelation of cosmic polarity—to render it powerless for materialistic and egoistic purposes by using forces that stream toward humanity from Gemini in particular, forces that can be made to serve the double.

As for other brotherhoods that want to avoid the Mystery of Golgotha, it is a matter of exploiting the twofold nature of human beings. This twofold human nature (which is within the fifth post-Atlantean period, just as we are) encompasses human beings as well as their lower animal nature. In a sense, human beings are really centaurs, since we embody a lower, bestial, astral nature; human qualities are somehow mounted upon this astral beast. This cooperation of our twofold human nature creates a polarity of forces. It is this polarity that will be more useful to the self-interested brotherhoods of the Eastern, Indian stream, who wish to mislead Eastern Europe in their task of preparing for the sixth post-Atlantean period. Forces from Sagittarius are used for this.

The question for humanity is whether to master cosmic forces in a way that is doubly wrong or to master them in the right way. This will lead to a real renewal of astrology, whose ancient form is a throwback and cannot continue. There will be a struggle in the cosmos among those who have knowledge. Some will use the morning and evening processes, as I described. The West will prefer the midday process and exclude the morning and evening processes; the East will use the midnight processes. Substances will no longer be prepared according to chemical forces of attraction and repulsion; it will be understood that different substances can be produced, depending on whether one uses morning and evening processes, or whether one uses midday or midnight processes. It will be understood that these substances will then have completely different effects on the trinity of God, virtue, and immortality, or gold, health, and prolonged life.

One will be unable to cause harm through the interaction of forces from Pisces and Virgo. Rather, one would, in a sense, loosen the life mechanism from the human being but not be able to establish any sort of power of one group over another. The cosmic forces thus utilized will lead to strange machines, but ones that will reduce human labor, since they will possess a certain intelligence. Cosmically oriented spiritual science will have the task of reducing harmful effects caused by the great temptations that arise from those mechanized beasts, which the people themselves have created.

And we must add something else to all this: it is necessary for people to prepare by seeing reality for what it is, not as illusions—by truly viewing the world in a spiritual way. It is important to see things as they exist. We cannot see things as they truly are, however, unless we are able to apply the ideas of spiritual science to reality. Those who have died will participate actively for the rest of earthly existence, and how they do this is the important thing. This is where the greatest distinction will appear. Through human actions on earth, the role of those who have died will be guided in a benevolent way, so that the impetus will be allowed to originate from those souls themselves, out of their own experience in the spirit world after death.

In opposition to this, there will be many attempts to lead those who have died back into human existence through artificial means. Through a roundabout path through Gemini, those who have died will be led into human life so that human vibrations will have a specific character and reverberate in the performance of machines. The cosmos will give movement to machines in the roundabout way I just described. Consequently, it is important that when such problems manifest nothing inappropriate be applied, but only elemental nature forces; people will have to avoid introducing inappropriate forces into technology. Esoterically, people must refuse to harness human beings to mechanical factory work, a system that uses the Darwinian idea of natural selection to determine the work force, as I described.

I cannot cover everything in such a short time, but I have presented these suggestions because I think you will meditate further upon them and try to build a bridge between what has been said and your own experiences—and above all, the experiences that are possible today during such difficult times. You will see that much will become clear to you by illuminating these matters in the light that comes through such ideas. Here, we are not really dealing with forces and groups of forces that confront one another—things constantly discussed in ordinary, exoteric life; we are concerned with entirely different issues. There are those who actually wish to veil the true impulses involved; there are always certain human forces that work to preserve something for themselves. But what is there to preserve? There are human forces working to defend impulses that were appropriate up until the time of the French Revolution, and they were even defended by certain esoteric schools. Now they are being defended in the form of an ahrimanic and luciferic reversion in an attempt to preserve a social order that people believe was displaced after the eighteenth century.

There are two main powers that oppose each other: those that represent the principle that was replaced at the end of the eighteenth century and those that represent the new age. It is clear that many people instinctively represent the impulses of a new era. The representatives of the old impulses of the sixteenth to eighteenth centuries must, therefore, be bound artificially to those forces that emanate from certain self-centered brotherhoods. The most effective way to extend power over the greatest number of people in the new age is through the principle of economic dependence. That is merely the means, however; something entirely different is also involved. You can deduce what this is from my various suggestions. This economic principle is connected entirely with creating a large human army from all over the world to fight for those principles.

Thus we have a polarity, a battle taking place in the world today. In the West, a rigid, ironclad principle of the sixteenth to eighteenth centuries, which clothes itself in revolutionary slogans, slogans of democracy—a principle that wears a mask while trying to gain as much power as possible. It helps when even a few people exert themselves to see things as they are, while most folks allow themselves to be lulled to sleep again and again in this realm by illusion. The illusion today is that there is a war between the centralized powers and the coalition for a common cause. In reality, this is not happening. We are dealing with entirely different facts, which exist behind this illusion as the truth. The struggle between the entente and centralized power is only an illusion. One can see what stands together in this struggle by looking behind these phenomena, thus illuminating them in the way that I have only hinted at for certain reasons. One must at least try not to accept illusion for reality, because this gradually dissolves the illusion—insofar as it must be dissolved. Above all, we must try to consider matters as they present themselves without preconceived notions.

If you coherently consider all that I have discussed here, then a seemingly chance remark in these talks will not be understood as merely incidental. It is not merely by chance but intended to illuminate matters when I quote a remark by Mephistopheles to Faust, "I see you know the devil, Sir, by heart" (and he never would have said that to Woodrow Wilson).[5] One must really study these things objectively, with an open mind. One must be able, above all, to reflect today about the meaning of a whole context of events and the meaning of individual strength, because behind the strength of individuals there is often something completely different from what lies behind the situation. Consider the question of how much Woodrow Wilson's brain would be worth if that brain were not sitting in the presidential seat of the United States. Imagine his brain in a different situation, where it would show its unique strength. It all depends on the situation.

I will now say something abstract and radical. Naturally, I will not expand on of the case I just mentioned; I would never think of doing this in such a neutral country. But aside from that, there is a very important insight into the question of the brain. Is its worth based on the fact that it is illuminated and animated by a particular spiritual soul force? Does it have a "spiritual weight" in the sense that I have used this term in our studies? Or would it have no more value than shown by physically weighing it on a scale? The moment one comprehends the mysteries I presented concerning the double, one brings real value to the brain (and I am not speaking of something unreal), which before had value only as a mass on a scale. One is capable, if the brain is to be revived, of allowing it to be revived merely by the double.

---

5. *Faust,* part 1, "A Gloomy Gallery."

Such things strike people today as absurd. What seems absurd, however, must become self-evident if these things are to flow in a healthy way. And what is the use of merely chattering about them constantly? You must realize that vague talk about "cosmic religiousness" or "the degree of the longing for it" or "the movement that wants to discover and reveal the movement of life behind the senses," and so on does nothing but place a smoke screen in front of facts that must become clear to the world. They cannot be effective without clarity, and, above all, they must be carried in clarity as practical, ethical impulses in human beings.

I can give only a few suggestions. I leave it to your meditation to build in these areas. These matters are aphoristic in many ways, but you will have the possibility of understanding a great deal from a summary such as this image of the zodiac, if you truly use it as the substance of meditation.

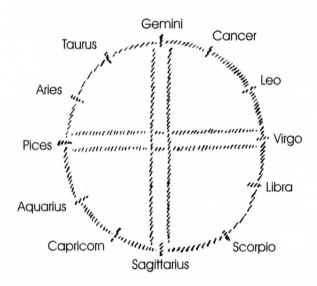

13 · The Three Realms between Death and Rebirth

Bern, November 29, 1917

Today I would like to return to the subject of an earlier talk here in Bern and pursue it further along the lines of what I believe we must discuss together.[1] It is clear to me that certain things required by the indications of our difficult times must be said in public lectures on Anthroposophy, so that they will penetrate human ears. I am also convinced that specific spiritual scientific truths must now be discussed among us.

In the lecture I mentioned, I described how souls who have gone through the portal of death continue to participate in earthly life. We studied the type and means of impulses from the so-called dead, souls who continue to participate in the activities of human beings on earth, and how those who are still alive can connect with those who have died. Today I want to say more about this.

First, it must be made clear that, during the life between death and rebirth, it is important for souls to be presented in some way with images taken from physical life on earth and

---

1. "How the Dead Influence the Living" (Bern, Nov. 9, 1916; GA 181), contained in Rudolf Steiner, *Staying Connected: How to Continue Your Relationships with Those Who Have Died,* (Anthroposophic Press, 1999).

from mental images acquired during physical life on earth. The nature of life in the world of the dead, however, is very difficult to understand through earthly concepts and mental images. Thus one must try to approach it in various ways.

I would like to say that one such attempt was made in a Vienna lecture course just before the outbreak of this world catastrophe [the World War].[2] I spoke about life between death and rebirth in relation to inner soul forces. Today, I would like to draw your attention to a subject that must, in some sense, become the primary concern of humankind in earthly life. The fact that this very subject is unavailable to the experience of souls who have died should be of primary concern to people. Consider how much we gain, as earthly human beings, through the mental images that come from the mineral and plant realms. Add to these, the mental impressions that come to us from heavenly space—the starry sky above, the sun, and the moon. Because these allow us to receive physical images in earthly life as perceptions, they belong to what I call mineral nature. This mineral nature and plants in their *essential* nature are not included in perception between death and rebirth.

Related to this is something especially characteristic of what the so-called dead experience. When we here on earth confront the nature of mineral or plant realms, we have a specific awareness. It is true that I said elsewhere that it is an illusion to believe there is no pain or pleasure in the mineral and plant realms. The results of our actions as human beings, however, make impressions on the mineral and plant realms; we can say with a certain justification that those realms have no such

2. See Rudolf Steiner, *The Inner Nature of Man and Our Life between Death and Rebirth* (Rudolf Steiner Press, 1994), 8 lectures and a short talk in Vienna, April 6–14, 1914 (GA 153).

impressions, unless such activities are spread by pain or pleasure, sorrow or joy. You know that, if a person smashes a rock, certain elemental beings will indeed experience pleasure or sorrow, but our ordinary, everyday consciousness does not experience this. Thus we can say that, in ordinary human experience on earth, we would never feel that we cause pleasure or pain in our environment by, say, breaking rocks or through some other activity in realm of minerals or essential plant nature.

This is not at all true of the realm we enter when we pass through the portal of death. You must be completely clear that there the slightest human action—even the barest touch (we must use the words of earthly language)—always arouses pleasure or sorrow in this spiritual realm; it arouses some degree of attraction or aversion. Thus you have to imagine that, in this realm of the dead, one's barest touch, even the slightest contact, causes the object that has been touched to experience pleasure or sorrow, attraction or aversion.

This was pointed out in my book *Theosophy*, which describes the realm of soul and sees its most important forces as those of attraction or aversion.[3] Such facts must become living ideas. As you become aware of the "interaction" between the realm of the dead and the realm of the so-called living, you must also picture how the dead function, so to speak, in their own realm. They function in such a way that they must always be aware that anything they do will evoke attraction or aversion, joy or sorrow; everything they do induces (if I may say it this way) a resonance of living sensation. What one might call the "insensitivity" of our plant and animal realms is not present at all beyond the portal of death.

---

3. See *Theosophy*, "The Soul World," p. 93.

In a sense, this describes the lowest realm that human beings enter when they go through the portal of death. When human beings come through the portal of birth into the physical realm, they enter the lowest domain, the mineral realm. When they enter the spirit world, human beings find themselves in a realm with a universal faculty for sensations, a realm where attraction or aversion rule. Within that world, human beings develop their forces; they work in that realm. When we imagine active human beings there, we must also picture the continuous forces that carry sensation from their actions, forces carrying attraction or aversion.

What is the significance of these forces within the entire web of relationships in the universe? You see, we have come to an issue that only spiritual science can resolve for our earthly life. You will understand the importance of this by considering all its implications. So much has come about these days that those who find the world explained only by physical means reject any other explanation as inconceivable.

In modern times, an example of such an explanation is the principle of how animal beings on earth evolved. I need only point to recent events to support the so-called theory of evolution. There is a certain justification today for the theory of evolution of the animal world, since it is believed that the animal world evolved up from imperfect beings to more perfect ones. A better way to express this would be to say that the animal world evolved from undifferentiated beings to greater differentiation, finally becoming human, insofar as humans are physical beings. This theory of evolution has already entered popular thinking to a great extent. In a certain sense, it has even become an aspect of the secular religion of humanity. The various religious faiths try to deal with this theory of evolution, but they (at least the more important representatives) no longer have the courage they had only a short time ago to testify against this theory of evolution. They have somewhat accepted it themselves and come to terms with it.

But now we could ask: If animal beings are evolving toward perfect beings, what is at work in this evolution? What is active in all that we see in the animal world, not just its evolution but its existence in general? As strange as it may sound to modern ears, upon entering the realm inhabited by the dead, through clairvoyant consciousness one discovers that the forces prevailing over most of the animal world are coming from the dead. Human beings are called on to help rule the impulses in the cosmos. In the mineral realm, human beings are involved only in what they build (such as machines) through technology, which follows the laws of the mineral realm. In the plant realm, it is a matter of planting and cultivating as gardeners or farmers. In these two realms, at best people take only second place during their life between birth and death. With the realm that animal existence mirrors here on earth, however, human beings are much more involved, because certain forces are immediately awakened in them after death, and they immediately enter and begin to work in a world of forces that rule the animal realm. It is a kind of foundation for human activity there, precisely as the mineral world is our foundation here; it is the very ground on which they stand.

In our physical existence, the plant realm rises from the ground provided by the mineral realm. Similarly, for those who have died, the foundation for a second realm is provided by the world of attraction and aversion, which extend into the life of animals on earth. In this second realm, the same things are not so much at work in the dead, the mere experiences of pleasure or sorrow, the transmission of merely sensation-bearing impulses that then continue, that then are active in the world. This second realm works essentially with what we can call the increase and decline of a person's will forces after death. To find more on those will forces, you can refer to the Vienna lectures, in which I pointed out that the will usually associated with the human soul between death and rebirth is not quite the same as the will during physical life.[4] Nevertheless, we can speak of it as "will," even though it is entirely different in that world, where it is permeated by elements of feeling and by an element that does not exist here on earth. The will of the human soul after death is in a constant ebb and flow. When one communicates with a human being who has died, that soul life is experienced in such a way that the will impulses feel stronger one moment, and the next feel weakened or even asleep; the will fluctuates between stronger and weaker. This is an essential quality of life for those who have died.

The strengthening and weakening impulses of the will, however, flow not only into the foundation of the realm of the dead but also into the human realm here on earth—not into the thoughts of ordinary consciousness, but certainly into all that we experience as will and feeling impulses.

It is strange, of course, that the ordinary consciousness of a physical person clearly experiences only sense perceptions and thoughts. Waking consciousness exists only in perception and thinking. Feelings are, in fact, only dreamed; we usually sleep right through it. People do not know what actually takes place when they simply raise a hand—when the will takes hold of the bodily organism—at least, not in the same way that people

---

4. Lectures 2 and 3 develop these ideas (see footnote on page 210).

know what happens during thinking. There is a similar characteristic of feelings: although feelings are somewhat clearer in consciousness, they are still dark—no brighter than the images of our dreams. Passions, emotions, feelings are really only dreamed; they are not experienced in the same light of consciousness that exists in sensory perceptions and mental imagery, and the human will is not experienced consciously at all.

Those who have died are alive in everything that plays into our waking life as dream or sleep. They live with the souls of those who are incarnated in physical bodies on earth. They live in them just as we live within the plant realm, except that we are not inwardly connected to the plant world as the dead are to our feelings, emotions, and volitional impulses; they live continually in all of this. This is their second realm. While here, our feelings and sensations unfold in human life, and the dead live continually in this life. Indeed, the alternating ebb and flow of the will of the those who have died has a certain relationship to the feelings and will impulses that the so-called living dream and sleep through.

You can see, therefore, how little the realm of the dead is separated from our earthly realm, and you can see the inner bond between these two realms. As I said, under normal conditions the dead have nothing to do with the mineral and plant realms (I will mention exceptions later), but they have much to do with activities in the animal realm; in a sense, it is the ground on which they stand. They are also related to what goes on in human feeling and volition. We are not separated from the dead at all in these realms, but it is like this: when we go through the portal of death and experience the increase and decline of the will, we are able to live with the so-called living in their physical bodies, though not with everyone. There a definite law prevails: one can live only with those to whom one has some degree of karmic relationship. One who has died does not even perceive a person on earth who is a complete stranger in terms of karma; the person simply does not exist. The world that the dead experience is bounded by the karma that limited them in physical life. This world is not limited to souls who are still on earth; it extends to those who have died.

This second realm thus embraces all the relationships that have been established karmically with those still on earth and with similar souls who have passed through the portal of death. This realm arises from another realm that is common to those who have died: a realm of animal existence (though we must not imagine earthly animals). I explicitly said earlier that earthly animals reflect what exists in the spiritual world—that is, the collective souls of animals. In relation to the dead, we must also think of the spiritual being of animals. From this common soil, then, an individual karmic realm arises for each and everyone who has died, though in an entirely different sense than is the case in our earthly realm. One person has made this relationship, another has made that one. Nothing is there from the human realm except what balances karmic relationships.

There is yet another law there; it shows us the makeup of this second realm. Initially, the ebb and flow of the will forces of one who has died are affected only by the human circle in which one moved during the previous earthly life—at first, perhaps only a part of it. Those who were especially close to that individual and who have died continue to live intensely with that soul. The circle gradually widens to include those with whom there was only a distant karmic relationships. For some, this lasts only a short time, for others longer. One can scarcely tell from the course of an earthly life how it will be after death. Many souls one would never have expected appear in the area of one who has died, because one can easily judge physical life incorrectly.

There is a fundamental law, however, that the karmic circle gradually widens. The whole process of becoming acquainted in this circle takes place exactly as I described it in the Vienna lectures dealing with life between death and rebirth. I described precisely this expanding life of will impulses as an important element in the life of the dead. For those who have died, will impulses become what mental images are for the living. Through them, the one who has died knows and has awareness. It is extremely difficult to explain in earthly terms that one who has died knows essentially through the will, whereas an earthly human being knows by forming mental images. Obviously, this also makes it difficult for the living to reach an understanding with those who have died.

Thus, one can say that this realm entered by the dead as their second realm widens gradually. Later, more distant karmic relationships are added to immediate ones; this is always relative and can happen sooner for one and later for another. I mean, after those who have died spend a certain time between death and rebirth, the circle of their experiences will have widened and stretched beyond the souls (whether on earth or beyond) with whom they have had particularly close karmic relationships. They now have karmic relationships apart from those of the ones who died. It is like this: A has a certain relationship with B but not with C. One sees how the dead person A lives with B (as I have described) and expands those experiences beyond B. Later, B becomes a go-between to person C. Previously A had no relationship to C, but now A enters that relationship directly through B's karmic relationship to C. Thus, the second realm slowly expands over a very large area. One becomes continually richer, as it were, through such inner experiences of strengthening or weakening the will, experiences that gradually accustom us to the realm of the dead—but living souls—after we have gone through the portal of death.

An essential aspect of life between death and rebirth is that, as souls, we increasingly widen our circle of acquaintances (to say it trivially). Here in earthly existence, we widen our experiences between birth and death by becoming acquainted with more and more of the world around us; similarly, there, our experiences increase and make us aware of the existence of other souls, and through some souls one experiences a strengthening of the will, through others a weakening. This is essential to our experience there.

You can understand the real significance of this for all cosmic existence. It means that there is a certain relationship between death and rebirth, forming a spiritual circle of acquaintances among a large portion of humanity around the earth—not just among the flavorless band that pantheists and mystics dream of and emote over. If we look at our experiences between death and rebirth, it is not all that far from earthly humanity. This is not abstract but a truly concrete connection.

On earth the animal realm is the third realm, just above the mineral and plant realms; likewise, across the threshold we also perceive a third realm, a realm of certain hierarchies of beings who never experience earthly incarnations, but with whom we come into relation between death and rebirth. Between death and rebirth, this realm of hierarchies across the threshold gives us our full experiences of I-being. Through the first two realms we experience the other; through the hierarchies we experience our I. One can even say that, as spiritual beings within the hierarchies, human beings experience themselves as children of the hierarchies. We know ourselves in relation to other human souls, as I have described; at the same time, we know ourselves as children of the hierarchies. Here, we experience ourselves within the cosmos—a fusion of outer natural forces and the surrounding cosmos; similarly, across the threshold we experience ourselves, as it were, organized as spiritual beings through the participation of various hierarchies.

Perception through Imagination can picture, in general, the course of life between death and rebirth. Indeed, it would be an extremely unhappy situation for those who could not create such mental images. Just consider: we are not separated from the dead at all in our feeling life or volition; that world is removed from our view and merely hidden from sensory perception and mental imagery. It will be a giant step forward in the earthly human evolution that we still must live through if one day people realize that they are united with those who have died through their feeling and will impulses. Death does in fact take away our physical view of those who have died, as well as of our thoughts of them. In everything we feel, however, those who have died are there with us in that realm in which we feel; likewise, in everything that we will, the dead are with us in our realm of volition.

If we observe ourselves as human beings (and this should certainly not lead to any pride in us), we see the so-called lower realms of nature and that we are placed at the peak of those realms. When we go through the portal of death, we find that we are on the lowest realm of the hierarchies, but as a fusion of impulses from the hierarchies. There, however, this fusion comes from above, whereas on earth it arises from below. In the earthly realm, our I is lowered into our physical organism so that it is really an extract of nature, but there our spirituality is embedded in the hierarchies as an extract of them. One can say, too, that there we clothe ourselves with our spirit nature, whereas here it is our physical nature with which we are clothed as we come through the portal of birth.

Earlier I mentioned exceptions regarding the mineral and animal realms. Such exceptions are especially likely during our present era; previously, they did not carry much weight, but we do not need to discuss this now. In our time, when a certain materialistic belief must spread over the earth, people can easily miss the opportunity to acquire spiritual mental pictures during their earthly lives. In yesterday's public lecture I even went so far as to point out how, if people fail to acquire spiritual mental pictures during earthly life, they chain themselves to this earthly life; in a sense, they will be unable to escape it, and they thus become a source of disturbance.[5] Many destructive forces at work in the earthly sphere come from those dead souls imprisoned within it. We need to have compassion for such souls and not judge them, because it is not very easy to be forced to remain after death in a realm that is really not suited to those who have died. In this case, they are the mineral and plant realms—the mineral realm that animals and human beings carry within. Such beings are permeated by the mineral realm. Those who have not taken in mental images of a spiritual nature shrink from this experience after death; feelings are always aroused, warning them that they cannot enter the worlds governing animal and human spirituality—that they

---

5. The lecture is not included in the bibliographic survey of Steiner's works.

can enter only realms of mineral and plant nature. I can scarcely describe this, because language has no words for it. One can approach the actual basis for this only gradually, because it is initially too frightening.

Do not imagine that these souls of the dead are permanently banished from the life I described earlier, but they approach this life with a certain dismay and fear; they repeatedly return quickly to the plant and mineral realms, since the mental images they constructed are meaningful only within the mineral realm of dead objects and physical mechanisms.

Today I consider it my primary purpose to arouse, through these imaginations, a conscious understanding of how the dead participate in human evolution. One would truly like to be able say these things in public lectures today, but this is impossible, since people will not accept such images unless they have gone through something discussed within our groups. By describing life between death and rebirth—especially in terms of earthly life—one fulfills today's need. For a long time now, people have discarded the ancient, instinctive imaginations of the world of those who have died, and now it is time for people to receive new imaginations. Humanity must be freed from abstract ideas about the higher worlds; people must cease to merely discuss spirit in a kind of general way. They must begin to actually perceive the activity of spirit. We must clearly understand that the so-called dead have not really died; they are still alive, and they are involved in the historical process of human evolution. We must be clear that the spirit forces around us belong to the higher hierarchies; they also belong to those who have died. The greatest illusion that people in the future could entertain would be to think that earthly society, which people develop themselves through their feelings and will, happens only through earthly arrangements, to the exclusion of those who have died. This is simply impossible, since the dead already participate in our feeling and volition.

How will it be possible to develop consciousness correctly— to perceive this association with the spirit world—amid new age impulses? Human evolution is proceeding in such a way that people, in their physical bodies and with ordinary consciousness, are increasingly cut off from the spirit world. The Mystery of Golgotha took place in earthly evolution so that human beings could once again—within the physical body— find the right access to the spirit world. The Mystery of Golgotha is not just an event that happened at one point in time; it is the greatest single event in all of earthly evolution, because it is a continuing impulse that is still active. Humanity must act, so that this force can work on human souls in the right way. For a long time I have stressed the fact that the purpose of spiritual science is related to the impulse of Golgotha; spiritual science must exist in a certain way so that the impulse of Golgotha can be correctly understood, both in our age and in the immediate future.

Natural science is an earthly science that has also become the religion of the world, and you can be certain that it will become increasingly influential. I am often blamed for being unfriendly to the natural sciences, even in their radical developments, but such reproach belongs to the most dated biases imaginable. Anyone who understands the course of earthly evolution also understands that the natural sciences cannot be proved wrong; on the contrary, they will only spread. A kind of religious belief in natural science is sweeping through the world, and it cannot be stopped; it is inevitable, progressing confidently "for the good of humanity." Soon, perhaps in the next few decades, the religions will all find themselves unable to save even the most simple, backward people from the limited consciousness of a strictly physical existence, as cultivated by natural science. This is a certainty.

It is also certain that, as the natural scientific worldview gradually takes hold of human sensibilities, it will be less and less possible for natural science itself to cultivate the spiritual element. The spiritual element must be developed in a strictly scientific a way, even as natural science continues to recognize only physical existence. Knowledge of natural existence will become more and more necessary so that, in the future, people will be able to fulfill their purpose between birth and death. Anything that will lift human beings toward the spirit world, however, will have to come from a spiritual science.

There is now a widespread and fundamental impulse to understand the Mystery of Golgotha. This could be seen in earlier times, but it is especially apparent now. As strange as this may sound, one can say that today's greatest enemies of such understanding are the priests and clergy of the various religions. People are kept furthest from the Christ impulse by the clergy and theologians themselves and the way they interpret this Christ impulse, because they are not even close to understanding its true nature.

It is not my intention today to speak of the essential matters regarding the Christ impulse. We have already said a great deal about it for some time now, and we will continue to do so. I would, however, like to present one aspect to you now, because it seems especially important at the moment. It is the fact that people must realize that, in the deepest sense, the Christ impulse must be approached very differently than one would other historical facts. People see this, but they constantly make all sorts of compromises. They speak half-truths and lack the courage for the whole truth. It must be understood that one cannot speak of the Christ impulse in the same way that people discuss ordinary history. Important theologians claim that it is foolish to speak of the Gospels as historically true in the ordinary sense, since everything they offer as historical proof that Christ actually lived can be written on a few sheets of paper. Well-known theologians today thus admit that it is useless to study the Gospels as historical documents; there is no way to prove that they represent historical facts. This is considered self-evident today. According to these famous theologians, a couple of sheets of paper could contain all of the historical proof—the sort one would write as authentic documents about other historic personages. What this really means, however, is that even what is written on those few sheets of paper is not true in the ordinary historical sense.

Humanity will have to acknowledge the fact that historical sources, such as those for Socrates or a Caesar, simply do not exist for the earthly life of Jesus Christ. His existence must be comprehended spiritually; this is the essence of the matter. Humanity will have to accept the fact that there are no physical proofs for the Mystery of Golgotha; it must be understood in a spiritual way. Humanity can always keep searching for historical proof of everything else, but, in the deepest sense, proof will never be of any use for the Mystery of Golgotha. People should not be encouraged to understand this important event on earth in the sense of physical history, but to approach it with spiritual understanding. Those who refuse to grasp the Mystery of Golgotha through a spiritual understanding of earthly evolution—without historical documents—will never understand it at all. This is the will of the gods, so to speak. Regarding the most important event on earth, human beings must exert spiritual activity. The Mystery of Golgotha can always be refuted historically; people will understand it only when it is raised to a spiritual comprehension of the world.

Only spiritual science can discuss the reality of the Mystery of Golgotha. One could say that everything else is out of date. Read the recent books of theologians; they are remarkable despite everything and develop all the "Jesus theories" of the new age, from Lessing to Wrede. You will find proof in such exegeses that history itself must take second place in this field; there must be a new kind of understanding, and this can be found only on the path of spiritual science.

We must understand this: now, in our time, the moment has come when human beings will truly be able to experience spiritually the continuing activity of the Mystery of Golgotha. This is why I have spoken of the spiritual, etheric reappearance of Christ in the twentieth century, and why I presented it in my first mystery drama. It will be a spiritual experience—a clairvoyant spiritual experience. Consequently, there is an inner relationship between the Mystery of Golgotha and the fact that humanity, beginning now, must ascend to spiritual cognition. From this time forward, people must rise to spirituality and understand that, in this coming time, the Mystery of Golgotha can be fully comprehended only through spiritual activity. Christianity can continue only in an essentially spiritual way; it cannot merely continue in an outer way through outer traditions and historical research.

I hope that what I have said will not be understood in an abstract sense and lead people to think that, if they pick up one or two ideas about the meaning of the Mystery of Golgotha, they have done everything necessary; it often happens this way.

People must instead approach these matters in a completely realistic way. One must not only build imaginations about the Christ and his activity; one must also be able to find, in a certain sense, the realm of Christ within the earthly world. Christ descended into the earthly realm, and one must be able to find his domain there.

If natural science is one day developed to its peak of perfection, it will present a picture of the world as it might have been without the intervention of the Mystery of Golgotha. During earthly evolution, natural science will never advance on its own to the point that physicists or biologists will be able to speak of the Mystery of Golgotha from their own logical deductions. Insofar as it deals with earthly events between birth and death, science will gradually become increasingly a science of nature. Along with this, spiritual science will draw its facts from the spiritual realm.

The question now, however, is whether we will find ourselves with only a science, or whether we can, in fact, stand within the spirit world and find ourselves with more than nature. We will never find the Christ impulse in nature, so how can we find a way to place ourselves within the spirit world and not just have knowledge of it? Based on what I have said, you can see that modern consciousness (as well as that of future humanity) will become merely an awareness of only natural facts, and you can see that another consciousness must be added to this, an entirely different awareness. The need to comprehend the Mystery of Golgotha as a spiritual fact will be only the "highest peak" of this new awareness. This approach needed for the Mystery of Golgotha—the willingness to get through to the spiritual element in phenomena—will have to extend throughout rest of life. This means simply that, beyond a purely natural view of the world, an entirely different view of phenomena must enter human consciousness. This view will arise once people learn to consciously observe the course of earthly destiny—in both the great and small events—just as people can now observe the physical world through sensory perceptions.

What does this suggest? People today pay little attention to the course of their destiny. Consider an extreme case, which I will relate to show you what I mean—and this is just one out of thousands; one could relate countless thousands. A man left his house to go for a walk along a path very familiar to him. It took him up a mountain to a rocky place with a beautiful view. He went there often to enjoy the view; it had become his usual walk. On that day, while walking a thought suddenly came to him out of the blue: "Watch out! Be careful!" He heard an inner voice—not a hallucination, but the spirit—saying, "Why are you going this way? Perhaps you could miss this pleasure just once." He heard this in spirit, making him hesitate and step off the path to think for a moment. Immediately, a tremendous mass of rock plunged over the very spot where he would have been if he had not stepped aside; it was clear that the rock would have killed him.

Now, please consider for a moment what the role of destiny was. Clearly, something was happening, and the man remained alive. The lives of many people on this earth are connected with his life. All of those lives would have been changed if the rock had killed that man. Something was accomplished. If you try to explain this according to natural laws, you could never comprehend the act of destiny that took place there. Of course, natural laws can explain how the rock came loose, how the man would have been killed as the rock suddenly fell on him, and so on. But the laws of destiny cannot be found anywhere in all that one can say about the matter from the view of natural laws; it has nothing to do with natural laws.

I gave you an extreme case, but our lives are composed of such things, insofar as our lives are a matter of destiny. People just fail to notice it; they pay no attention to these things. People do not notice such events in the way they do events conveyed through the senses as natural facts. Every day, hour by hour, and moment to moment, events such as this extreme case take place. Consider, for example, how often you are about to leave home and are delayed perhaps half an hour (we must even look at the small events). Such things happen thousands of times during our lives. You see only that delay of half an hour and fail to consider what might have happened if you had gone out as scheduled, half an hour earlier.

Thus another, different realm continually reaches into our lives—the realm of destiny, still ignored by people today, because they look only at events as they have happened, having no interest in the events that are prevented in their lives. Not one of you here can know whether, maybe three hours earlier, some event was prevented that might have kept you from being here tonight—perhaps even kept you from being alive right now. You see only the results of spiritual impulses that gathered in manifold ways and, through which, an event took place. With ordinary consciousness, you do not generally consider the fact that whatever you do in life is the result of participating spiritual impulses. Once you begin to comprehend this fact and realize that a realm of destiny exists, just as a realm of nature exists, you will find that this realm of destiny is essentially no less real than is the realm of nature. What I described earlier works into this realm of destiny—a world that reveals itself with particular clarity when some extreme incident occurs, like the one I related, thus becoming obvious to the human intellect. The impulses of those who have died enter the feelings and volition through which destiny works. Despite the fact that people who say such things are still seen as superstitious fools by today's so-called intelligentsia, one can nevertheless say, with the precision of a natural law: whenever someone hears such a voice, it belongs to one who has died, speaking at the prompting of a spiritual hierarchy. Furthermore, from morning until evening—and even more so from evening until morning while asleep—the impulses of those who have died work into us continually, along with the impulses of spiritual hierarchies at work in our destiny.

Now I would like to mention something else. You know about the daimon of Socrates, that wise Greek, and what he said about it. He said that everything he did was influenced by his daimon. I spoke of this Socratic daimon in my small book, *The Spiritual Guidance of the Individual and Humanity.*[6] In my recent book *Riddles of the Soul,* the second chapter speaks of the learned Dessoir, and you can see what he had to say about such things.[7] There I pointed to Socrates' daimon, and how it was a matter of his becoming aware of something at work in everyone. Prior to the Mystery of Golgotha, certain beings directed what the dead would bring to human life. Those beings lost their power with the event of Golgotha, to be replaced by the Christ impulse. Now the Christ impulse is bound to human

---

6. *The Spiritual Guidance of the Individual and Humanity: Some Results of Spiritual-Scientific Research into Human History and Development* (Anthroposophic Press, 1991; GA 15), p. 23. On the daimon, see also Steiner's *Christianity As Mystical Fact* (Anthroposophic Press, 1997; GA 8), chapters 2–3.

7. *Riddles of the Soul* (Mercury Press, 1996; GA 21). Max Dessoir (1867–1947), a German philosopher whose main focus was esthetics. He was also interested in parapsychology.

destiny as described by spiritual science. The forces and impulses of the dead work into the sphere of our will and feeling, as I have described. The dead are active, but they also experience strengthening or weakening of their own will. That whole world is an earthly realm, like the realm of nature. Since the Mystery of Golgotha, however, the Christ impulse is living within it; Christ is the directing power in the realm I described.

This must go beyond mere abstract truth to be recalled occasionally. It must go beyond concepts or "Sunday truths," simply because, after all, something like this might actually be true. People should walk through this realm of destiny as consciously as they walk through the realm of sensory perceptions. People should be able to go through the world while using their eyes, and yet they should also have the sense of being woven right into the realm of destiny. People should be able to feel that, within this realm, the forces of Christ are always united with the forces of those who have died. If this were really the situation today, humankind would develop in itself a real, concrete, and sensitive life with those who have died. People would experience something or other while engaged in some activity, and would feel united with loved ones who have passed on. Life would become endlessly enriched.

Thus, people will have to establish a science based on the Mystery of Golgotha. It will have to become known in the future that, just as the world of natural facts permeates our world, likewise a realm of destiny permeates it as the opposite pole. The realm of destiny is scarcely noticed today, but it will have to be studied in the future just as fully as is the world of nature. When this is done, people will know that, within the realm of destiny, we are connected with those who have died. People will realize that the world we share with the dead is also the realm of Christ. The Christ descended to earth to reveal his influence through the Mystery of Golgotha, to show earthly humankind what we have in common with the those who have died, insofar as they are active within the earthly sphere. I am not talking about exceptional events, but ordinary ones.

People today do not completely forget those who have departed; we hold them in our memory. The only true life will be an intense life; otherwise people will sleep through life, insofar as destiny is concerned. This intensity will take hold of human beings so that they not only remember those who have died, but know that when they work toward a goal, and when success is achieved, the soul of someone who has died is participating. Our connections with the dead are by no means severed by death; they continue. Such an enriched life is the prospect for humanity in the future of earth. In this fifth post-Atlantean epoch, humanity is in fact evolving in the direction I am describing, and humankind will certainly be unable to survive the sixth epoch if people do not begin to feel these things in the right way, taking the reality of destiny into their consciousness just as fully as people today absorb the reality of natural phenomena. We must perceive the very real connection between the Mystery of Golgotha and the matter of death.

This is what I wished to point out today. It must now enter human consciousness, because, among the many things lost by humanity, it is still possible to experience true reality in our feeling and will impulses. Human beings have been lulled gradually into the grand illusion that this earthly life can be shaped according to earthly laws. This is the greatest illusion that people have fallen into. We find the ultimate expression of this, for example, in purely materialistic socialism, which sets up everything according to economic principles—that is, according to purely physical laws. Obviously, socialist materialism would never accept the idea that, whenever we do the smallest thing among ourselves, the dead are participating. Socialism is one extreme; the opposite extreme is the dream of every "idealist" today: to create, with no regard for anything spiritual, organizations throughout the world, both domestic and international, purely for the purpose of promoting programs to end all war. It is impossible to convince those who cherish such illusions that they cannot eliminate war in this way—that, instead, they themselves adopt the very monster they wish to destroy. There is plenty of good will in such efforts. This is simply what must emerge from the materialistic consciousness of this time; it comes, I would say, as the political peak of the whole essence of the world today.

Those efforts will lead to the exact opposite of the desired effect. A true understanding of destiny is the important development that must spread over the earth. It must take hold in legislation and in the formation of political parties; it must provide the very foundation of society. Anything incompatible with the spiritual evolution of humankind will simply dissolve; it will break down or wear out. This is closely connected with the signs of the times today. We do not need to get involved in political campaigning (if I may be so blunt), but naturally we would not do that anyway. Nevertheless, those who care about the spiritual evolution of humanity must carefully note the needs of today. It must be understood that the Christ will only be lost along the road most commonly traveled today. He will be won as the true king and lord of the earth only when people ascend along a spiritual path. You can be sure of this: Christ cannot be found as the various religions look for him today— faiths that, remarkably, have already given in to every possible compromise for understanding the Christ. Here and there, religions have even agreed on ways to celebrate the Christ as a god of slaughter. People must look for the Christ where he can be found in reality—as we have suggested today—by understanding that Christ can be found the realm of destiny. Only then will a world organization be created that can significantly spread true Christianity over the earth.

Just reflect for a moment, and you will realize that we have not yet reached this goal. Consider what would happen if you approached those who speak of establishing world peace—and who doesn't talk about it—and offered a program to make Christ available to humanity. Peace would indeed come, lasting peace, insofar as this is possible on earth. Imagine the response if you presented such a program to those peace organizations (created, I grant you, out of sincere good will). We have even experienced a "peace program" emanating from "Christ's representative on earth." You will not find there, however, much of Christ. I know that these things are not taken seriously enough today, and, unless they are, humanity will be unable to follow a healthy path. It is necessary to understand the Mystery of Golgotha on a spiritual level, and it is equally necessary to clearly understand the signs of the times and that, without spiritual science, even the outer structure of future society will not emerge.

· Further Reading

RUDOLF STEINER

According to Luke: The Gospel of Compassion Revealed, Great Barrington, MA: Anthroposophic Press, 2001.

According to Matthew: The Gospel of Christ's Humanity, Great Barrington, MA: Anthroposophic Press, 2003.

Anthroposophical Leading Thoughts: Anthroposophy As a Path of Knowledge, The Michael Mystery, London: Rudolf Steiner Press, 1998.

Anthroposophy and Christianity, Great Barrington, MA: Anthroposophic Press, 1985.

The Apocalypse of St. John, London: Rudolf Steiner Press, 1993.

At Home in the Universe: Exploring Our Suprasensory Nature, Great Barrington, MA: Anthroposophic Press, 2000.

Background to the Gospel of St. Mark, London: Rudolf Steiner Press, 1985.

The Bhagavad Gita and the Epistles of Paul, Great Barrington, MA: Anthroposophic Press, 1971.

The Book of Revelation: And the Work of the Priest, London: Rudolf Steiner Press, 1998.

The Bridge between Universal Spirituality & the Physical Constitution of Man, Great Barrington, MA: Anthroposophic Press, 1958.

Building Stones for an Understanding of the Mystery of Golgotha, London: Rudolf Steiner Press, 1985.

Christ and the Human Soul, London: Rudolf Steiner Press, 1972.

Christ in Relation to Lucifer and Ahriman, Great Barrington, MA: Anthroposophic Press, 1978.

Christianity as Mystical Fact, Great Barrington, MA: Anthroposophic Press, 1996.

The Christian Mystery, Great Barrington, MA: Anthroposophic Press, 1998.

The Easter Festival in the Evolution of the Mysteries, Great Barrington, MA: Anthroposophic Press, 1987.

An Esoteric Cosmology, Blauvelt, NY: Garber Communications, 1987.

The Evolution of Consciousness, London: Rudolf Steiner Press, 1991.

The Fall of the Spirits of Darkness, London: Rudolf Steiner Press, 1993.

The Fifth Gospel: From the Akashic Record, London: Rudolf Steiner Press, 1995.

Freud, Jung, & Spiritual Psychology, Great Barrington, MA: Anthroposophic Press, 2001.

From Buddha to Christ, Great Barrington, MA: Anthroposophic Press, 1978.

From the History & Contents of the First Section of the Esoteric School, 1904–1914, Great Barrington, MA: Anthroposophic Press, 1998.

From Jesus to Christ, London: Rudolf Steiner Press, 1973.

The Gospel of St. John, Great Barrington, MA: Anthroposophic Press, 1984.

The Gospel of St. John and Its Relation to the Other Gospels, Great Barrington, MA: Anthroposophic Press, 1982.

The Gospel of St. Mark, Great Barrington, MA: Anthroposophic Press, 1986.

How Can Mankind Find the Christ Again? Great Barrington, MA: Anthroposophic Press, 1984.

How to Know Higher Worlds: A Modern Path of Initiation, Great Barrington, MA: Anthroposophic Press, 1994.

The Inner Nature of Man: And Our Life between Death and Rebirth, London: Rudolf Steiner Press, 1994.

Intuitive Thinking as a Spiritual Path: A Philosophy of Freedom, Great Barrington, MA: Anthroposophic Press, 1995.

Learning to See into the Spiritual World: Lectures to the Workers at the Goetheanum, Great Barrington, MA: Anthroposophic Press, 1990.

Life between Death & Rebirth, Great Barrington, MA: Anthroposophic Press, 1968.

Life beyond Death: Selected Lectures, London: Rudolf Steiner Press, 1995.

Love and Its Meaning in the World, Great Barrington, MA: Anthroposophic Press, 1998.

Materialism and the Task of Anthroposophy, Great Barrington, MA: Anthroposophic Press, 1987.

The Mystery Dramas: The Portal of Initiation, The Soul's Probation, The Guardian of the Threshold, The Soul's Awakening, London: Rudolf Steiner Press, 1997.

Mystics after Modernism: Discovering the Seeds of a New Science in the Renaissance, Great Barrington, MA: Anthroposophic Press, 2000.

The New Spirituality and the Christ Experience of the Twentieth Century, London: Rudolf Steiner Press, 1988.

An Outline of Esoteric Science, Great Barrington, MA: Anthroposophic Press, 1998.

Polarities in the Evolution of Mankind: West and East, Materialism and Mysticism, Knowledge and Belief, London: Rudolf Steiner Press, 1987.

Pre-Earthly Deeds of Christ, North Vancouver, BC: Steiner Book Centre, 1976.

The Presence of the Dead on the Spiritual Path, Great Barrington, MA: Anthroposophic Press, 1990.

Rosicrucian Wisdom: An Introduction, London: Rudolf Steiner Press, 2000.

The Souls' Awakening: A Mystery Drama, Great Barrington, MA: Anthroposophic Press, 1995.

The Spiritual Guidance of the Individual and Humanity, Great Barrington, MA: Anthroposophic Press, 1991.

Staying Connected: How to Continue Your Relationships with Those Who Have Died, Great Barrington, MA: Anthroposophic Press, 1999.

Theosophy: An Introduction to the Spiritual Processes in Human Life and in the Cosmos, Great Barrington, MA: Anthroposophic Press, 1994.

The True Nature of the Second Coming, London: Rudolf Steiner Press, 1971.

A Way of Self-Knowledge, Great Barrington, MA: Anthroposophic Press, 1999.

OTHER AUTHORS

Thomas, Nick, *The Battle for the Etheric Realm: Moral Technique and Etheric Technology: Apocalyptic Symptoms,* London: Temple Lodge, 1995.

Urieli, Baruch Luke & Hans Müller-Wiedemann, *Learning to Experience the Etheric World: Empathy, the After-Image, and a New Social Ethic,* London: Temple Lodge, 1998.

· Notes on the Lectures

This collection was originally edited by Gilbert Church and Alice Wulsin. All translations have been revised for this edition.

"The Appearance of Christ in the Etheric World," January 25, 1910, Karlsruhe (GA 118), translated by Barbara Betteridge, revised;

"Spiritual Science and Etheric Vision," January 27, 1910, Heidelberg (GA 118), translation revised;

"Buddhism and Pauline Christianity," February 27, 1910, Köln (GA 118), translated by Diane Tatum;

"Mysteries of the Universe: Comets and the Moon," March 5,1910, Stuttgart (GA 118);

"The Reappearance of Christ in the Etheric," March 6, 1910, Stuttgart (GA 118);

"The Sermon on the Mount and the Land of Shambhala," March 15, 1910, Munich (GA 118);

"The Return of the Christ," April 18, 1910, Palermo (GA 118), translated by Ruth Pusch;

"The Etheric Vision of the Future," May 10, 1910, Hannover (GA 118), translated by Ruth Pusch;

"The Etherization of the Blood," October 1, 1911, Basel (GA 130);

"Spirit Beings and the Ground of the World," November 18, 19, 25, 1917, Dornach (GA 186), translated by Margaret de Ris and Alice Wulsin;

"The Three Realms of Life Between Death and Rebirth," November 29, 1917, Bern (GA 182), translation by Alice Wulsin.

During the last two decades of the nineteenth century the Austrian-born Rudolf Steiner (1861–1925) became a respected and well-published scientific, literary, and philosophical scholar, particularly known for his work on Goethe's scientific writings. After the turn of the century, he began to develop his earlier philosophical principles into a methodical approach to the research of psychological and spiritual phenomena.

His multifaceted genius led to innovative and holistic approaches in medicine, science, education (Waldorf schools), special education, philosophy, religion, agriculture (biodynamic farming), architecture, drama, movement (eurythmy), speech, and other fields. In 1924 he founded the General Anthroposophical Society, which has branches throughout the world.